The Revolution
in Education

MORTIMER J. ADLER

and MILTON MAYER

The Revolution
in Education

With an Introduction by Clarence Faust

 THE UNIVERSITY OF CHICAGO PRESS

Library of Congress Catalog Number: 58-5534

THE UNIVERSITY OF CHICAGO PRESS, CHICAGO 37
Cambridge University Press, London, N.W. 1, England
The University of Toronto Press, Toronto 5, Canada

© *1958 by The University of Chicago. Published 1958*
Composed and printed by THE UNIVERSITY OF CHICAGO
PRESS, *Chicago, Illinois, U.S.A.*

Preface

This book attempts to locate the major differences in theory and principle which underlie the current acute controversies about American education—about its purposes, its institutional arrangements, and its methods. It does not, its authors point out, seek "to find the right answers; it is trying to find the right questions."

It assumes that the clarification of the basic issues in current educational controversy might not only clear the air but open the way to more fruitful discussion of the alternatives open to American education in the twentieth century. Certainly, in much of current controversy about education opposing parties never really join issue. Each party describes the positions of its opponents in terms its opponents refuse to accept, and each views the criticism of its opponents as merely the demolition of straw structures.

Whether Mr. Adler and Mr. Mayer's analysis of the issues in the present debates about education goes to the heart of the matter each reader will of course judge for himself. The book will have served its purpose if he either finds the analysis illuminating or is led to attempt another formulation which identifies the views of opposing parties in ways both would accept as doing justice to their positions.

The book is an outgrowth of material prepared for a seminar session several years ago of the members of the boards of the Fund for Adult Education and the Fund for the Advancement of Education. The method it employs has been and is being applied to other critical problems, such as the idea of freedom, by the Institute for Philosophical Research, of which Mr. Adler is director.

The interest these days among educators and laymen alike in the questions of policy and practice in American education, which has mounted so rapidly in recent years that educational controversy has become front-page news, must be encouraging to all who believe in the critical importance of education to the way and quality of American life.

This book seeks to find a way of inducing, in the widespread controversies which are already well under way and bound to become more insistent, at least as much light as heat.

CLARENCE FAUST

Contents

PART I

The Few Become the Many

CHAPTER 1

American Revolution, 1850–1950

The mass of our citizens may be divided into two classes—the laboring and the learned. . . . At the discharging of the pupils from the elementary schools (after three years of schooling) the two classes separate—those destined for labor will engage in the business of agriculture, or enter into apprenticeship to such handicraft art as may be their choice; their companions, destined to the pursuits of science, will proceed to the College.

These words are among the most revolutionary ever written. They proposed—in the year 1814—that every American child go to school. For only three years, to be sure; but in 1814 the proposal was revolutionary, not only in America, but everywhere in the world.

The words were written by an old hand at revolutionary documents, Thomas Jefferson. They appear in a letter to his nephew, Peter Carr, a letter outlining Jefferson's projected "Bill for Establishing a System of Public Education." And it may be debated which of the two documents—this one or the Declaration of Independence, inscribed by the same hand—was the more revolutionary. Never before in the history of the world had a great statesman proposed universal free education.

Less influential men had made the proposal in ages past. The Czech philosopher Comenius wrote in his *The Great Didactic* in 1632: "All who are born to man's estate have need of instruction, since it is necessary that, being men, they should not be wild beasts, savage brutes, or inert logs. And since all have been born with the same end in view, namely that they should be men, it follows that *all* boys and girls, both noble and ignoble, rich and poor, in all cities and towns, villages and hamlets, should be sent to school." Jefferson, too, was only a private citizen when he wrote Peter Carr; but he was the First Citizen of the land, and he had fought for education in season and out. In 1813 he reminded John Adams of his earliest effort a generation before:

. . . At the first session of our [Virginia] legislature after the Declaration of Independence, we passed a law abolishing entails . . . [and another] abolishing the privilege of primogeniture. . . . These laws, drawn by myself, laid the ax to the foot of pseudo-aristocracy. And had another which I prepared been adopted by the legislature, our work would have been complete. It was a bill for the more general diffusion of learning. This proposed to divide every county into wards . . . ; to establish in each ward a free school for reading, writing and common arithmetic; to provide for the annual selection of the best subjects from these schools, who might receive, at the public expense, a higher degree of education at a district school; and from these district schools to select a certain number of the most promising subjects, to be completed at an University, where all the useful sciences should be taught. Worth and genius would thus have been sought out from every condition of life, and completely prepared by education for defeating the competition of wealth and birth for public trusts. . . . Although this law has not yet been acted on [more than thirty-five years later], I have great hope that some patriotic spirit will, at a favorable moment, call it up, and make it the key-stone of the arch of our government.

As we read these words today, they are tame—indeed, "re-actionary"—so far has Jefferson's revolution in education pro-ceeded. They did not contemplate the schooling of girls or of the children of slaves; they restricted universal schooling to the most elementary level; they did not involve compulsory at-tendance. Compulsory instruction in reading and religion had existed for a century in Calvinist New England—the first com-pulsory education in the English-speaking world—but it had passed with the passing of township theocracy. Jefferson him-self opposed compulsion, asserting in connection with his Bill for Public Education that "it is better to tolerate the rare in-stance of a parent refusing to let his child be educated, than to shock the common feelings and ideas by the forcible aspor-tation and education of the infant against the will of the father." The first state to adopt compulsory education at public expense was Massachusetts in 1852, and Jefferson's own Virginia did not require attendance until 1908.

The proposal of free elementary schooling for all (even on a voluntary basis) was the beginning of the democratic revolu-tion in education, a revolution now matured in our own and most other Western countries. Contemporaneously with Jef-ferson, Pestalozzi in Switzerland had been urging the free education of the poor, and compulsory schooling on a fee basis was on the statute books (if sporadic in practice) in both Scot-land and Prussia. The demand for free public education for all children was as revolutionary in mid-nineteenth-century Europe as it had been in America a century earlier; it was made by Marx and Engels in the *Communist Manifesto* in 1848, "to win the battle of democracy."

Neither the Declaration of Independence nor the United States Constitution mentioned education. The nation's first statement of public policy on the subject was made in the Northwest Ordinance, enacted in 1787: "Religion, morality, and knowledge being necessary to good government and the happiness of mankind, schools and the means of education shall ever be encouraged." The Ordinance provided that one thirty-sixth of each township in the new territory be set aside for the maintenance of schools. But it was a long way from the *encouragement* of public education to its *requirement*.

The way was long because the United States of Jefferson's time was neither a political democracy nor an economic democracy, as indicated in Jefferson's distinction between "those who are destined for labor and those who are destined for learning and leisure." America had rebelled against England in 1776, but the revolution within America did not begin until later. The American republic of the eighteenth century resembled the Greek republics of the time of Plato in two fundamental respects: economically it was non-industrial, and politically it restricted citizenship. So—as in all the past centuries of Western history—education was for the few leisured men, destined for the life of learning or for public or private professions or the heights of trade and commerce. It was not for the many who labored, who were destined for a life of toil in a society moved not by machines but by human muscle.

The very difficulty of comprehending this concept nowadays indicates how radical the American revolution of 1850–1950 has been. The word "school" derives from the Greek word for leisure, σχολή. This term, *scholé*, came to mean, in ancient Greece, a learned discussion or dispute, which those with time for leisure, and they alone, could engage in, and, finally, the place where such discussion or dispute took place. Leisure did not (in Greece or in Jefferson's America) mean idleness; it meant, on the contrary, intense and sustained intellectual activity—the hard work of the liberal arts and sciences and the onerous duties of citizenship and statecraft. It could be enjoyed only by those who had enough economic freedom from unremitting manual toil to acquire learning and use it. It meant the opportunity to come to think like, talk like, even live like (or, at the very least, *look* like) a gentleman; Henry Adams was of the opinion that he had learned "self-possession" and nothing else at Harvard. He was a member of the class of 1858.

The man of leisure might impose upon himself the most onerous duties imaginable, he might work harder all his life than the meanest laborer, but having free time was the prerequisite for his voluntary engagement in such leisure-work. The connection is implicit in Jefferson's animadversions on sending American youth to Europe for education; in 1785 he wrote:

What are the objects of an useful American education? Classical knowledge, modern languages, chiefly French, Spanish, and Italian; Mathematics, Natural philosophy, Natural history, Civil history, and Ethics. In Natural philosophy, I mean to include Chemistry and Agriculture, and in Natural history, to include Botany, as well as the other branches of those departments. It is true that the habit of speaking the modern languages cannot be so well acquired in America; but every other article can be as well acquired at William and Mary college as at any place in Europe. When college education is done with, and a young man is to prepare himself for public life, he must cast his eyes (for America) either on Law or Physics. For the former, where can he apply so advantageously as to Mr. Wythe [professor of law at the College of William and Mary]? For the latter, he must come to Europe: the medical class of students, therefore, is the only one which need come to Europe.

There was nothing incongruous in the statement of the great eighteenth-century radical, Rousseau, that the poor needed no education at all. Why should men (much less women!) who lived and died in the sweat of their labor be sent to school? Why, above all, should the state, in whose governance they had no role, send them? Sentimentalists—and revolutionaries like Jefferson—might call for public education and demand the establishment of schools maintained at public expense for children whose parents could not afford private tutors or pay the fees of the schools of the time. But a more respectable view than Jefferson's was voiced by the governor of neighboring South Carolina: "The free school system has failed. . . . The paupers for whose children it is intended need them at home to work." (These free "pauper schools" were essentially apprenticeship institutions.) Outside Calvinist New England and New York, there was no general demand to make free education available, much less compulsory. Western Massachusetts was a long way from Boston—or from Athens. Kentucky was a longer way still.

The keystone was not to be set in the arch in Jefferson's time. It awaited the American revolution of a century later. Before the need of universal education could be argued effectively in the country, the character of both political and economic life had to be changed. The United States had to move by extension of the franchise—in 1868 to ex-slaves and in 1920 to women—toward the democratic ideal of universal suffrage, and machinery had to replace (or at least reduce) the leisureless burden of those who would be enfranchised. As long as citizenship meant only trial by jury, immunity from search, and the like, the citizen's educational condition did not appear to be of crucial importance to the state. But when citizenship came to mean the determination of public policy at the polls, ignorance could at last be seen as a public menace which the state, to preserve itself, had to avert by providing schooling to those who would not get it otherwise.

But the governor of South Carolina could not be gainsaid; as long as the pre-industrial economy obtained, parents needed their children's labor. Resistance to public school attendance was as ardent—and often violent—among the poor as it was among those who, financially able to educate their children at home or in private schools, resented being taxed to educate the children of "paupers." Whether or not child labor was a moral curse, it was accepted, in pre-industrial America, as an economic necessity. Massachusetts, in inaugurating compulsory school attendance in the middle of the nineteenth century, did not dare to require more than twelve weeks a year, only six of which had to be consecutive.

The second American revolution—or the two revolutions, political and productive—did occur. Their Fourth of July was July 28, 1868, when the Fourteenth Amendment to the Constitution enfranchised every male citizen. The shift of productive power from muscle to machine was already proceeding at a spectacular pace. In 1840 less than 5 per cent of the power used in this country was supplied by machines, the rest by men and animals; today 84 per cent is supplied by machines. And in less than fifty years, from 1840 to 1888, school attendance increased 520 per cent, those in school rising from 119 to 196 per thousand persons of the rapidly growing population. In one decade alone, 1870–80, illiteracy was cut in half, from 16 to 8.1 per cent of the population over the age of ten. There were five times as many high schools in 1890 as there were in 1870.

A fully developed industrial democracy is something new in human history. The revolution of the past century in America may leave man and society substantially unchanged, in so far as man remains man and his society human society; but it is a revolution that has invalidated the answers to many of the questions which stood, questions and answers together, for all the preceding centuries. No man had dreamed of an age in which all men would be citizens who had to be educated, all of them possessed of the leisure in which they could assert the birthright of man to mental development.

Educational theories and practices before the middle of the nineteenth century may not be irrelevant to the problems of education in our day, but they cannot solve those problems. Contemporary problems have got to be solved in terms of a social organization which nowhere existed in all the preceding twenty-five centuries of Western history. To say that the challenge is appalling suggests at once that every age, with understandable hyperbole, is appalled by the novelty of its situation. But our age is objectively unique, at least in this one respect. Never before have the men who thought about education had to think about educating a whole people.

We have *had* to think about it. The idea of democracy properly horrified the ancients because the state would be governed (as indeed some states were, from time to terrible time) by a mob of uneducated men. Democracy, said Thomas Hobbes in the seventeenth century, was "government by orators" appealing to the passions of men who did not reason. Why not teach men to reason? Sir William Berkeley, colonial governor of Virginia, gave the monarchist answer in 1671: "I thank God that there are no free public schools and printing and I hope we shall not have them for three hundred years, for learning has brought disobedience and heresy and sect into this world and printing has divulged them and libels against the best government. God keep us from both."

When the "best government" of Hobbes and Berkeley gave way to republicanism and then, a century later, republicanism gave way to industrial democracy, a new *kind* of society had to hammer out new educational practices and (what is much harder) new educational principles as well. To be sure, the practical problems of education have always been hard to solve, however well established the principles. Every society in every epoch in history has had to confront the relationship of education to its religious and political institutions, to its economic system and the economic condition of its people, and to its social traditions and the general culture of the society at a particular stage of its historical development. But none has had to face the problem in such radically changed circumstances as ours.

It is not that our practical problems are difficult (though they are). If they were only difficult, we could turn with confidence to the experience of the past. It is that they are new. In certain critical respects our situation cuts us off from the past altogether. We may call upon it, perhaps with profit, as we find our way, for its whole experience is that of men in society and we are men in society; but we must find our own way. The forces which produced political democracy and industrial production revolutionized the quantitative problem of education. They also evoked two qualitative changes which, educationally, themselves represent a break with the whole past. One of these changes is the secularization of society. The other is what might be called its scientization.

For the first time since the end of the sixth century there is a general system of education that has no connection of any kind with religion or the church. This is a modern—even recent—development, and it is not unique to the United States. But in spirit it grows everywhere from the conditions that gave rise to the European settlement of this continent: a demand for freedom of worship and the consequent plurality of religious communions within a single national society. And nowhere is the plurality of communions as extensive and divergent as in this country.

The America of Jefferson's time was still a devout society, and Jefferson himself assumed that religion and natural theology would be taught in the public schools and that the various communions would be encouraged to establish their institutions of worship and instruction in the immediate vicinity of the public educational establishments: "The relations existing between man and his Maker, and the duties resulting from those relations, are the most interesting and important to every human being." But Jefferson's hopes of peaceful coexistence between education and religion were not to be realized. The general dread of a state church and the mutual hostility of the religious denominations were too strong, and today public education is completely (if sometimes uneasily) separated from religion.

The second qualitative change in society—taking place simultaneously with secularization—has been its increasing focus on science and technology and the specialization arising from that focus. This has been in the making since the late seventeenth century, but it is only within the last fifty years that its full impact has been registered on education, especially in the United States but also in Germany, the U.S.S.R., and other countries. We live in an age of science, an age of specialized research and production dominated by the scientific method and by the fruits and promises of technology. This fact has influenced the content, the method, and the aims of education at every level down to the kindergarten. It has influenced the organization of secondary schools, leading to the development of the technical or vocational high school and to the rise of the junior high school and the junior college. And it has completely altered the organization of higher learning, both in teaching and in investigation. For the advancement of learning in an age of science, specialization in study and research has become the rule. The number of professions or vocations requiring specialized training has been multiplied by the progress of technology and the consequent intensification of the division of labor.

Whether or not a close connection exists between the secularization of society and its "scientization" is a question of importance and dispute, but it is not central to the mere description of our situation and the problems which that situation poses. These two qualitative changes in society, revolutionary in themselves, have shifted the emphasis, spirit, organization, content, and method of American education. And they are problems in addition to the quantitative problems induced by industrialization and universal suffrage. If we had enough schoolteachers and schoolrooms—if, in a word, the present "educational crisis" were past—the real educational crisis of what to teach, how to teach it, and with what purposes would be full upon us.

Qualitatively even more than quantitatively, we find ourselves on the near side of the great watershed of social history. The conditions of much of human society, while they have never been static, have been turned upside down and inside out in the past century, and nowhere as radically as in the United States (except, of course, in Russia, where the change, much more rapid and much less organic, has been from and to conditions different from our own). After the American War of Independence, Jefferson's fellow fighter for public education, Dr. Benjamin Rush, said, "The revolution is not over." He might have said that it had not yet begun. The history of education, as we look back at it from this side of the watershed, reveals a general stability during all the earlier ages. What is education in an industrial democracy in an age of science? This is a new question.

CHAPTER 2

Ancient Questions—and Answers

There were, in the centuries that preceded 1850, great crises in education, but there was still greater continuity. The pre-scientific, pre-industrial societies—sacred or secular—were concerned with the schooling of the few and with them alone. The polity might be a republic, an aristocracy, an oligarchy, or even a tyranny; its basic concern was the same: to prepare the leisured few for the learned or holy vocations and, in later times, for the highest ranks of commerce and government. The pattern was no more altered by the phenomenon of the student beggars of the Continental universities at the end of the Middle Ages than it was by the English "charity schools," the pre-Revolutionary "pauper schools" in America, or the appearance of an occasional hayseed at Henry Adams' Harvard.

The two great educational crises of the ages past were not

educational crises at all but religious. The first occurred with the transition from Greek and Roman antiquity to pre-medieval Christendom. The ideal function of education in the Greek city-states was defined by Plato in the *Republic* and the *Laws* and was practiced in greater or lesser degree before and after his time: the preparation of the elite few for the service of the state and its governance. The absolute supremacy of the state may have been worse abused in later ages, but it has never been better praised than it was in ancient Greece. Lycurgus, the lawgiver of Sparta, was, so Plutarch recites, "of a persuasion that children were not so much the property of their parents as of the whole commonwealth." Accordingly, "he bred up his citizens in such a way that they neither would nor could live by themselves; they were to make themselves one with the public good, and, clustering like bees around their commander, be by their zeal and public spirit carried all but out of themselves, and devoted wholly to their country." So single-minded was their education that they were not allowed to learn of governments different from their own. Some four hundred years later Aristotle was glorifying the Spartans for making education "the business of the state." "The citizen," he said, "should be moulded to suit the form of government under which he lives . . . if the laws are democratic, democratically, or oligarchically, if the laws are oligarchical."

This classic doctrine had its echoes a few decades ago in the cry of "adjustment." The business of education was the adjustment of the child to his environment. But the "adjustment" school—or, at least, its slogan—passed from favor with the rise of the modern totalitarian state whose educational system adjusted the child to an environment which Americans thought abominable. Then came the second World War and the Cold War, and Aristotle, and even Lycurgus, were heard again. "The overarching objective," says Dr. Wilbur A. Yauch, chairman of the Department of Education at Northern Illinois

State Teachers College, "the objective for which schools primarily exist, is to indoctrinate for democracy."

The Spartans, the Athenians, and later the Romans espoused indoctrination of the young in the name of education partly to ward off subversive ideas and partly to secure the state, through the will and training of its citizens, against attack from without. In the face of the Communist threat the role of education in national security has come to the fore in our own time, as many of the speakers at the 1955 White House Conference on Education indicated. Citing the Soviet Union's lead in training scientists and engineers, Vice-President Nixon told the Conference that "it is apparent that our national security has a tremendous stake in our educational system." Neil H. McElroy, then president of Procter and Gamble Company and chairman of the President's Committee for the White House Conference (and subsequently Secretary of Defense of the United States) went further: "In this highly technical era, education has become as much a part of our system of defense as the Army, the Navy or the Air Force. We must have good schools, not only because of our ideals, but for survival."

Another participant in the Conference was worried by the integration of education into the survival of the state. Speaking on "What Should Our Schools Accomplish?" President James R. Killian of the Massachusetts Institute of Technology said: "In Nazi and communistic societies there isn't much doubt about that question—their schools are arranged to shape youth to the needs of the state. It is of course a tradition in our own country to consider the individual paramount; we would not think of subordinating the educational desires of an individual to the needs of the state. . . . And we cling to this freedom for the individual even though it looks at times as though the welfare of the nation were suffering from it."

"For instance," President Killian went on, "we need science teachers in our schools today even more desperately than we need other kinds of teachers, but there is no way in which we can impress students into programs which would prepare them to be science teachers. . . . In an age when science is essential to our safety and our economic welfare, it might be argued that a shortage of science teachers and of scientists and engineers is a clear and present danger to the nation. I, for one, am convinced that it is just that."

Presumably, Nazi and Communist education—and Greek and Roman—would sacrifice freedom to the national danger. President Killian thinks it is not necessary: "Personal opportunities are often created by national needs—the national shortage of engineers has led to good jobs for young engineers and, as a consequence, can bring about an increase in the number of students seeking training as engineers." President Killian's hope might be realized, but what if there were a national shortage of, say, sonnet-writers or saints, and the job market did not respond by raising salaries in those professions? The question has been asked before. Plato thought the state was short of philosophers, for whom personal opportunities were scarce and wages low. He offered the classical answer—which in principle seems to be the Nazi and Communist answer: Man belonged to the state, and education was to mold him to its service and survival.

The revival of the ancient doctrine under modern stress is still attacked. As long ago as 1917, with England at war, Bertrand Russell, in his *Why Men Fight*, excoriated the "molding" principle of education as the highest treason to the child: "What is considered in education is hardly ever the boy or girl, the young man or young woman, but almost always, in some form, the maintenance of the existing order. . . . Hardly anything is done to foster the inward growth of mind and spirit." And Canon Bernard Iddings Bell, in the midst of Cold War, wants the university to be "a breeding place of rebels, a sender forth of graduates who, unadjusted and unadjustable, would try to turn the world upside down"; a far and forlorn cry from the reaction to the successful launching of the Soviet Union's earth satellites in 1957, when Americans in high quarters and low called for an all-out effort by the educational system to overtake the totalitarians' lead in the production of scientists and engineers for national defense.

The aim of education remained the same throughout antiquity: to "mold" the good man and the good citizen, the two being generally held identical. The means were the inculcation of patriotism or the service of the state, the cultivation of the intellect, and (to whatever degree it might be achieved through schooling) the discipline of the passions in the direction of the classical ideal of moderation. But the school did not exist as we know it, and, until the last few centuries of Rome, it did not exist in any form. Instruction was private, or in very small groups, and peripatetic. In a world where nearly all labor was done by slaves, the students were members of that minority destined by birth or fortune (usually by both) to live a life of leisure or, in any case, of intellectual and not necessitous toil.

But Athens and Rome did not wholeheartedly follow the utopian precepts of Plato and Aristotle and make education "the business of the state." The young citizen's father directed his education and sent him with a specially designated slave, a παιδαγωγός, a "child-accompanier," from which the word "pedagogue" is derived, to hear lectures. The Romans placed more (and, in earlier periods, all) of their emphasis on the father's education of the son, directly and as supervisor of the teaching slaves (who were usually Greeks). The home was the school, and family example the primary tool of instruction. In the first century A.D., Quintilian (who kept a school of rhetoric and is sometimes called "the first public school teacher" because he was the first whose wages were paid by the emperor) grievously lamented the withering-away of familial education.

Whatever adjustments were made in content and method from place to place and epoch to epoch in the ancient world, the curriculum that evolved was substantially the same. It consisted of what Cicero called "the liberal arts" of grammar (including folk literature), logic or dialectic (the art of argument), and rhetoric (the art of persuasion, which included law and lawmaking). These, plus geometry (including geography and natural history), astronomy, arithmetic, and music, were distinguished as the arts of liberty or the life of freedom, the political freedom of the citizens or ruling class and the economic freedom of the leisured to engage themselves in political, intellectual, or aesthetic activity. They were the arts (in contrast with the "servile" or mechanical) that freed man from the ignorance to which the slave was condemned by the conditions of economic production to perform his primitive labors.

Religion played an increasingly perfunctory role as classical culture developed, except in times of public crisis. At their height the pagan civilizations of the northern and eastern Mediterranean treated their gods ceremonially, as symbolic representations of the state and its prowess; and the symbolic representations of the state, in turn, were deified. The golden eagles of the Roman legions "were placed in a chapel in the camp," says Gibbon, "and with the other deities received the religious worship of the troops." Of course mythology—combining religion and education—was integral to the education of the child. But theology as we know it was non-existent, and philosophy had no concern with the antics of the gods.

Far from repudiating the Greco-Roman construction of education—based on the liberal arts—the early Greek Fathers of the Church, such as Clement and Origen, regarded Christianity as a kind of ultimate philosophy. An uneducated man might be a Christian, but liberal education was the means of actually understanding the mysteries of faith. Even Augustine and Jerome advocated the liberal arts, whose ends were worldly, insisting only that they be subordinated to the Christian life, whose ends were other than worldly. It was not until the Middle Ages that the cleavage between the two objectives was sharpened into a revulsion against the intellectualism of pagan education isolated from Christian faith. But the liberal arts, preserved through the Dark Ages in the monasteries, were never rejected; with a religious foundation beneath them, they continued to dominate the medieval curriculum as they had the classical. The continuity of Western education was not interrupted by the religiously oriented schooling of medieval Christendom.

The Renaissance broke the religious pattern of the Middle Ages but not the educational continuum that began in Greece and Rome. On the contrary; re-emphasizing the secular ends of classical humanism, the Renaissance accepted the education of antiquity, rejecting only the aim of the service of the state as it rejected the medieval aim of the service of God. But the schools—such as they were—were rooted in the church, and, in spite of the progressive secularization of the university curriculum and the opening of schools under civil control in the Hanseatic towns in the fifteen and sixteenth centuries, nearly all schooling remained in the care of the churches for another three hundred years. The churches, originally interested in augmenting the priesthood, always provided an educational opportunity for a limited number of poor boys; such a purpose in part motivated the establishment of Winchester, Eton, and St. Paul's in England between the fourteenth and sixteenth centuries. But the motivation was soon lost or submerged, and the schools became aristocratic. Education remained, from the Renaissance to the second quarter of the nineteenth century, in America no less than in Europe, the prerogative of the advantaged few, its graduates trained for the highest affairs, its basic content that of late antiquity plus religion variously emphasized in various periods.

To say that education remained substantially the same for twenty-five centuries is not to say that there was unanimity in educational philosophy. Nor does it mean that great variations, in both theory and practice, did not appear from place to place and from time to time at the level of the organization of schooling or its duration, the method of instruction, or the exact content of the curriculum. Nearly all the great contributors to educational thought and action disagreed in respect to one or another of these issues. But they agreed on the fundamental convictions which maintained the continuity, from age to age, of the insights of Greece and Rome.

There were exceptions, of course, among educational philosophers, but the marvel is that among men whose general philosophies were incompatible (men like Aristotle, Augustine, Montaigne, Erasmus, and Benjamin Franklin) there were so few dissents from the prevailing philosophy of education. The list of exceptions is pretty well exhausted by Rousseau's emphasis upon naturalism and the cultivation of the instincts and, less radically if no less prophetically, by Locke's and Spencer's advocacy of vocational training in connection with general schooling and Bacon's plans for intensive specialization at the university level. But these dissents did not seriously affect educational practice during the centuries in which they were voiced; they have appeared in general practice only during the last hundred years.

The common practice—and the common theory—of every age preceding our own reduces, in summary, to five fundamental concepts. Upon these the institution of education rested undisturbed in Western history up to the middle of the last century.

First, the aim of education is the cultivation of the individual's capacities for mental growth and moral development. It is intended to help him acquire the intellectual techniques and aesthetic sensibilities, the knowledge, understanding, and wisdom requisite for a good human life spent publicly in political and professional action and privately in the worthiest use of leisure. As a secondary function, which it shares with other institutions, it concerns itself with the training of the body and the maturation of the emotions; this last objective (inculcated in part by rational emphasis on the "golden mean" and in part by discipline and personal concern) is viewed as a contribution to moral development. Specifically Christian education, of course, orients all these temporal objectives to the life of grace.

It was thought, in the second place, that basic schooling, given these objectives, must be "liberal" education. The corollaries of this concept were, generally, that basic schooling is the same for all who go to school, with due allowance for the varying dispositions of the normal individual; that training in the particular skills required for productive tasks is outside the area of basic schooling and is best acquired by apprenticeship; and that specialized education, after the completion of basic schooling, is to be given in only those vocations that are essentially liberal in character—namely, the learned professions.

Third, it was thought that education does not end with the completion of schooling, even of professional schooling, but, rather, that the pursuit of knowledge involves the effort of a lifetime and is one of the principal activities of those with time for leisure-work. Adult education was rarely discussed as such, partly because the stages of schooling were not so sharply defined by age level as they are now and partly, no doubt, because its pursuit, among the leisured few, was (correctly or incorrectly) assumed. But it was explicitly maintained that only the beginning of education can occur in youth because of the limitations intrinsic to immaturity and the limitations of any subject matter appropriate to immature study. To Seneca's dictum that "an old man who has still to learn his lessons is a shameful and ridiculous object; training and preparation are for the young, action for the old," Aristotle replies (three hundred years earlier!) that child prodigies may be found in mathematics and harmony, but never in morals or politics, which require the experience of life for their comprehension.

The fourth fundamental concept of education down the ages was that the profession of teaching is not only a learned profession, involving special preparation in the liberal arts and the skill of transmitting them, but also a profession of learning, in which the teacher not only practices his art but improves it by the continuous study of the subjects he teaches. The teacher is a lifelong learner.

Finally, the advancement of learning, upon which the vitality of education in any society depends, requires scholarship, or investigation and research, apart from the dissemination and acquisition of the learning already available; and scholarship is likely to flourish in a community of scholars (whether or not they are organized as the faculties of educational institutions) co-operating and comunicating across the separate fields of learning which, since their common goal is truth, are implicitly related to one another.

These concepts are enumerated as five for the sake of discussion here; they might be condensed or extended. What is important is that, historically, they represent together the basic principles of educational theory and practice of every epoch preceding our own. They were education's answers to the questions asked of it by the social situation of twenty-five prescientific and pre-technological centuries, in which what was required of education was to produce a small class of educated men. The differences and disagreements which arose in theory and in practice occurred within the general framework of these suppositions.

The fact that almost all educators and educational philosophers concurred in these general principles does not establish their validity. The fact that it was Cicero or Aquinas or Kant —or all of them together—who held these views does not mean that they were right. What it does mean is that they were held, and nearly universally held, by the best minds we have known from age to age. They do not, for that reason, command our assent, but they do command, in the name of common humility, our consideration.

Anyone who undertakes to judge their validity—for their time and place—has to consider one stupendous historical fact: These are the principles upon which the men responsible for our culture were educated, generation after generation, century after century. They are the principles upon which Plato taught Aristotle in Athens and Mentor Graham taught Abraham Lincoln in Sangamon County, Illinois. For better or for worse, this is the outline of the education which (to whatever extent education civilizes) gave us our civilization.

Among these thinkers, for all their agreement, the effectiveness of education as a civilizing agency was moot, as it still is and, it seems probable, as it always will be. The question asked in the first recorded discussion of education has not been answered: "Can you tell me, Socrates, whether virtue is acquired by teaching or by practice . . . or in what other way?" Schooling, which is what we are here concerned with, is only a part of the civilizing (or educational) process; it is that part dealing formally and primarily with the cultivation of the mind and only indirectly with the formation or fortification of moral character.

The Platonic adage that "the city educates the man" sobers the enthusiast for more and better schooling. There are other forces at work—the home, the church, the organization of society and the form of government (and the government itself), the streets and the playgrounds, and in a modern society the newspapers, magazines, and books (including comic books), and the cinema, the radio, and the television screen. These, too, are educational agencies in the general sense of the term. So are the economic order and the conditions of labor, housing, diet, and medical care. So are the genes and chromosomes; we are the omnibuses, said Oliver Wendell Holmes, in which our ancestors ride, and sometimes one of them sticks his head out the window and makes a terrible fuss. The school—in a word—is just *one* contributor to the education of men.

Of this particular institution the free man is the end product. While there are certainly such men who have not been schooled, the purpose of liberal education is to contribute to the production of such a man. We may agree that moral training is central to the development of the free man, but whether such training is within the primary competence of the institution of secular education is arguable; not, however, here. What is unarguable—at least historically—is that the direct and overt objective of liberal education is the liberation of the intellect from ignorance and its cultivation as a critical instrument.

The wisest men of whom we have record agreed generally that the principles upon which education was conducted up to a century ago better fulfilled the limited objective of such education than any other principle or set of principles. Were we living today in one of the many societies in which they lived, we might follow their consensus with confidence. But we are not. We are living in a society which none of these men of imagination ever imagined.

CHAPTER 3

Modern Questions

However imperfectly the ideal of universal suffrage is realized in the United States—and it is realized more perfectly every day—its embodiment in the basic law of the land makes "every man a king," every American adult the sovereign ruler of the state, holding, like the king he is, its highest and only permanent office, that of citizen. But the king must be educated, and he must be educated to rule. A truly democratic state without compulsory education at public expense would be an anomaly. Universal education is an inescapable corollary of universal suffrage.

With the emancipation of the chattel slaves came their enfranchisement a few years later. With their enfranchisement came the desperate necessity to convert them from their condition of general illiteracy to one of adequate education. Southern demagogues—and many other men, thoroughly sincere—argued against emancipation on the ground that, even if slavery were morally indefensible, the country would not survive the ravages of uneducated freedmen at the polls, and on this point the Great Emancipator agreed with them. Nor would it have, for long; the freedman had to be given the educational opportunity of a ruler.

In 1920 almost half the adults in the United States became, for the first time, full citizens: the women. They had, of course, played a progressively freer role in society for a century, and their status was reflected in the changed character of "female education," which was steadily becoming indistinguishable fom that of the adolescent male. In all ages past, women, along with slaves, had been foreclosed from liberal education. In Jefferson's time no American college admitted them. The first college for women (Wesleyan Female College, in Macon, Georgia) and the first college to become coeducational (Oberlin College, in Ohio) have the same founding date —1837. Previously, girls of the wealthy class were instructed by private tutor or in seminaries or finishing schools in reading, writing, and ciphering for household management, in cooking, needlework, and music, and sometimes in the care of minor medical emergencies in the home. Since the adoption of the Nineteenth Amendment and the removal of the last disabled segment of our people from political ineligibility, the lines between "male" and "female" education have disappeared.

It took almost two centuries to establish in this country the principle of free education for every future citizen and almost a century more before our people agreed that schooling had to be the full-time occupation of the child and that even eight years of elementary education were insufficient for his preparation for intelligent citizenship and the blessings of private life. But then the change was rapid. In 1875 there were only 500 high schools in the United States, and in 1900 this country had a smaller proportion of its population in school than any country of western Europe except Italy. But in 1925 there were 16,000 high schools, and in 1950, 71.3 per cent of all American children between fourteen and seventeen years of age were in school. In 1900 there were about 500,000 boys and girls in all the high schools of this country, or about 10 per cent of those who were eligible. Today there are over 7,000,000 or approximately 85 per cent of all the children between fourteen and seventeen years of age. No other country attempts to give secondary schooling to more than 20 per cent of its youth.

The school-leaving age rises every year now; today almost as many high-school graduates now go on to college as do not. Under conditions of advanced industrial production, the campaign for child labor laws and a child labor amendment to the Constitution has subsided, except in very limited areas; mechanization, which in its early stages produced the frightful torture of children in factories, mills, and mines, has finally produced, in anything like normal conditions, an adult labor "surplus" that makes child labor unnecessary even in non-moral terms. Automation promises to make the whole adult population "surplus labor" in increasing degree. Under present and presently projected conditions of industry, it is economically possible from a manpower standpoint for compulsory basic schooling to be lengthened to a fourteen- or even sixteen-year period; the absorption of eighteen-year-olds into the peacetime army did not retard production.

Along with the reduction of labor time, the industrial economy has vitiated the age-old distinction between a leisured class and a laboring class. With exceptions that are rapidly becoming spectacular, every adult is both a worker and a man of leisure. Not only are the idle rich disappearing, but it is not in the least uncommon, where the five-day week prevails, to find the employer working longer hours than his employees. What is more, under public and private pension systems the employer is likelier than his employee to go on working in his advanced age. The divisions of American society today—and no one supposes that the direction of change will be reversed—are no longer divisions into distinct classes. They are, rather, a division of the time of every adult into distinct activities—those of labor and those of leisure, the one devoted to wealth or the goods of subsistence, the other devoted to the creation of civilization or the goods of the human spirit.

The increase of time available for leisure activities with the shortening of the work day, the work week, and the work years has opened the possibility of continuing education to almost every adult who wants it. The adult education movement in this country once had two primary purposes—first (still common in Europe), to provide opportunity for adults to make up for insufficient basic schooling in childhood; second, to orient non-English-speaking immigrants. With the lengthening of the period of compulsory education and the closing of mass immigration, there is less and less need for compensatory or orientation schooling for adults. Adult education tends now to become the kind of education which sustains and advances learning after adequate basic schooling has been completed in youth.

With the political, productive, and scientific revolution of the past century fully developed, the problems of education in mid-twentieth-century America can be seen by examining the realities of the present against the background of one fairly reliable assumption about the past, the assumption that the traditional principles of education (enumerated in the preceding chapter) were valid for an undemocratic, non-industrial, and pre-scientific society. Acceptance of this assumption leads at once to the two questions upon which the discussion of our present problems may be sharply focused: Are the traditional principles valid for a modern industrial democracy, with, of course, such adaptations as contemporary circumstances indicate? And if they are not, what is now to be the meaning of education and its fundamental aim and procedure? The serious educational controversies of the last two or three generations —the generations that have begun to feel the full impact of the great change in society—have revolved around these two questions.

If the traditional principles are valid, and by one or another means adaptable to modern conditions, certain subordinate questions are immediately raised. Do we know how to apply them so that what was once the education of the few can be made the education of all? Can the teacher, under the increased pressures of the modern profession and of modern life, be expected to go on learning? Can the community of scholars that was once thought to be an indispensable condition for the advancement of learning coexist with intense specialization in an era of science and technology?

And if the traditional principles are held to have been valid under past historical conditions, but no longer, to what criteria are we to turn for the judgment of alternative principles? What is the ideal to be substituted for the liberal education of the few who were to be free and responsible citizens, when every man and woman is to be free and responsible? What kind of men and women (in so far as education contributes to their development) do we want in order to maintain and perfect the kind of society we want, and how may education proceed to contribute to their development?

The extremist view—that the traditional principles were invalid even for their own time and irrelevant and even misleading for ours—is matched at the other extreme by the view that the traditional principles of education can be applied whole, without amendment or adaptation, to our new kind of society. This view, like its equal and opposite, is rarely advanced in contemporary discussion. In between, the two more moderate positions more or less adequately embrace those who have made a sustained and conscientious effort to think about education for our time.

Each of the two moderate positions has a different obstacle to overcome. The first, or traditionalist, position must discover and formulate the means whereby the same quality of liberal education that was once the privilege of the few can be extended to all, both in school and (given the advance of leisure) in adult life. The second, or non-traditionalist, position must redefine the aims of education to conform to the realities of an industrial democracy in an age of science, but without making it any less appropriate for all the men who are now citizens and men of leisure than the education of past ages was for the ruling few of the leisure class.

As we examine current educational controversy of an earnest—rather than a polemical—nature, we are likely to find that the two moderate positions are not wholly irreconcilable. This does not mean that there are not basic disagreements among the protagonists. It means only that their disagreements might be more manageable if they were seen in the light of their common rejection of both the extremist positions. Unfortunately, the educational literature of the last fifty years has, in bulk, tended to foist each of the appropriate extremes upon each of the moderate positions. The consequence has been more conflict than controversy. The character of the conflict has not only obscured the real issues; it has diverted attention from them, and especially the attention of each side from the difficulties of its own position. The chance of surmounting these difficulties—and of solving the problems of education in a scientific and industrial democracy—might be greater if the problems themselves could be clarified.

True, even when the disputants are well behaved, each making every effort to understand the other, the main lines of the controversy tend to blur as the major positions come to grips with particular problems, such as the age at which basic schooling should be completed, or the organization of the successive parts of the school system, or the relation of vocational to nonvocational subjects, or the kinds of materials to be used in teaching them. True, too, these and the problems like them are the actual problems, and the only actual problems, that confront educators from day to day in *this* school in *this* community. The purpose of this book is not to solve (or to pretend to solve) such problems but to state them; to trace them to the much larger issues from which they spring, issues which, in the press of practical administration, are ordinarily unseen and unconsidered; to formulate the lines of major controversy about those issues and to locate the points of convergence and divergence of the controversialists; and to suggest the direction or directions in which we might look for the possibility of resolution. This book is not trying to find the right answers; it is trying to find the right questions.

The real differences in philosophy of education in our time are the consequence of the social revolution of 1850–1950. In the face of that revolution education could not continue in its historic forms. It could not, and it did not. The forms fell apart, or were burst by the forces generated by the democratic, industrial, and scientific revolution in America. Education went on, in any and every which way. Both of the moderate positions in the current controversy call for principled reforms in the prevalent practices of the schools, and for this reason both of them are opposed, or, rather, blindly rejected, by those (not all of whom are outside the field of education) who do not wish to be disturbed.

But they are being disturbed, willy-nilly. Parents are challenging the popular practices—or demanding to know exactly what they are and what they are for. Civic organizations are challenging them. Even pupils are, in their own often inarticulate way, challenging them by "delinquent" behavior. In the midst of the hullabaloo, harried schoolmen, who did not bargain for all the criticism the schools are getting, are heard saying plaintively that they have troubles enough without being asked, "Why?" and "What for?" The motto of all old institutions is, "Don't rock the boat." A distinguished Englishman once said that in educational reform the time is never ripe until it is rotten.

There is another, perhaps more tangible if less potent, source of opposition to both moderate positions. The traditionalists and the non-traditionalists accept the revolution of the past century and welcome it. They stand together against those who do not, against those who think either that democratic government is wrong or that the dispersion of the fruits of technology and industrial production, in the form of higher living standards and increasing leisure for the whole of our people, is deplorable. Democracy and mechanization of labor are here, and they are here together. Whatever their shortcomings in practice, they present the human race for the first time in human history with the possibility of the good life for all men and the equitable organization of human society.

The demands which modern democracy makes upon education cannot be avoided. To meet these demands in our own country—the most radically transformed of all modern societies—educational philosophers cannot bicker indefinitely. The problems are critical, and they must be faced with a view to their resolution in the best interests of our country and its people and their form of government and their aspirations. Businessmen and poets can, if they are financially independent, refine their techniques to their hearts' content before they go into production. Educators cannot; they are "producing" members of society whether or not they are ready to.

There is more, much more, at stake in educational controversy than the preservation of a point of view at any cost or the maintenance of prestige and position in an area of argument which, perhaps because educators are so often on the defensive in an activist culture, sometimes degenerates into polysyllabic fishwifery. Education needs to know what it is doing and why, and to be aggressive about it. "The keystone of the arch of our government," Jefferson called it. What the thinking of the past was able, at its best, to do for a society of some, the thinking of the present must try to do for a society of all.

PART II

The Lines of Reasoning

CHAPTER 4

What *Is* Education?

The men who were educated before 1850 were pre-democratic, pre-industrial, and pre-scientific men. But they were men. The society in which they were educated was a society of men. To say that our situation is radically different from theirs is not to say that the educational problems of men in society have no continuing common character. Whatever, wherever, whenever the society, the ultimate framework of educational discussion remains the same, because man, whatever his vicissitudes, remains man, with his human potentialities and limitations.

Education is, at all times and places and under all conditions, a peculiar combination of nature and art. Learning is natural to man. He learns by experience and discovery from both the human and the non-human events in his environment, and he learns also by instruction of an intentional and methodical character known as teaching. Both kinds of learning are obviously natural to him, and their product, the altered condition of the learner, who moves from ignorance or error to knowledge, is a natural product. But it is also a product of art.

Education shares this fundamental peculiarity with two other human enterprises—agriculture and medicine. In all three cases nature unaided aims at the end result—in agriculture, growth; in medicine, health; in education, knowledge. But in all three cases the artist, be he farmer, physican, or teacher, co-operates with nature to achieve the result of the natural process. Thus the teacher's function, however differently it may be delineated in one sort of society or another, is a co-operative, not a creative, function. He cannot make a silk purse out of a sow's ear—or (no matter how inept his teaching) vice versa. If a boy has an I.Q. of 84, the teacher cannot make an Einstein of him, for the teacher is an agent of nature; but he can help him become as much of an Einstein as a boy with an I.Q. of 84 can be, for the teacher is also an artist.

It is the fact that the teacher is an artist and not just a blind agent of nature that gives education the third common element of its character in any society. It is not only a natural process and an artistic undertaking, wherein one human being learns faster and better because of the assistance of another; it is also a practical enterprise. As a simple combination of nature and art, it involves only "Mark Hopkins at one end of a log and a boy at the other," one helping another to learn. But seen in terms of any society above the primitive level, it involves a special class of persons professionally engaged as educators in the service of their fellow men.

The essence of education is human association, of adults with children and of adults with other adults. It is, therefore, in any well-developed society, one of the greatest of all social enterprises. A school system, including all its institutions, offices, rules, customs, and procedures, is society's practical effort to maintain and improve the peculiar combination of the natural and artistic processes of education.

This elementary analysis acquires immediate relevance when we approach educational controversy according to its customary division into three parts: (1) the ends or objectives of the enterprise; (2) the institutions designed to serve those ends; and (3) the methods to be adopted for the purpose.

THE ENDS OF EDUCATION

Any consideration of objectives will involve all three aspects of education discussed above—nature, art, and practical social undertaking. The natural endowment of humans is clearly such that the objectives of education can never be final; it is wholly unlikely that the process can ever be made so complete as to render the individual incapable of further learning. Seen as an art, education (in the limited sense of schooling) aims at the production of distinguishable parts of the total result or objective which nature pursues; "all men want all good things," and education is designed to help them get the goods of knowledge. And as a practical undertaking it is limited by both the natural capacities of learners and teachers and the society's available artistic resources (teachers, equipment, the amount of the child's time to be allotted to schooling, etc.).

So divided, controversy over the ends of education seems to involve two related questions. First, what are the specific objectives that, taken together, constitute the end at which education in all its aspects (nature, art, and enterprise) aims? (For example, the development of the individual's physical, emotional, moral, social, or domestic capacities or, even more specifically, the development of particular capacities or skills.) Second, what are the different kinds of education (if there are different kinds) to be used to achieve the objectives sought, and can they be distinguished according to the specific objectives? (For example, moral and intellectual, general and specialized, liberal and vocational teaching.)

THE MEANS OF EDUCATION

When we turn to the institutional means, we at once encounter more obvious distinctions, three in number. The largest is between the school system commonly conceived as an institution for the education of the young and the institutions or agencies of adult education, the two being distinguished according to whatever distinctions may be made between immature and mature persons as learners. Within the school system commonly conceived, the differentiation into primary, secondary, and collegiate institutions is also made on the basis of the supposed stages of maturation of the learner. And the division of adult institutions or agencies as liberal, professional, and vocational presupposes a distinction of kinds of education appropriate to mature persons under existing social conditions.

The second problem is the relationship of one educational institution to another. While the connection between the school system as a whole and adult education is involved here, the much more familiar question is that of the connections among the different levels of the school system and among different kinds of schools. This question embraces the scope and duration of each level and kind of schooling, the conditions of admission to each, and the transition from one to another.

The third problem of means is the relationship of educational institutions—of whatever kind or at whatever level—to other institutions or agencies of society which, while they are not established for educational purposes, can and do perform educational functions: the home, the church, the library, the press and other mass media, the trade union, and the business, social, or professional organization.

THE METHODS OF EDUCATION

The last great area of controversy, after objectives and means, is method. Here the debate of the past half-century is hottest, in part, at least, because of the confusion introduced by the very real relationship of method and objective. Method comprises the curriculum or course of study intended to achieve the established objective and a great deal more. The skills or techniques of teaching belong to method, and so, of course, does the external apparatus used, such as books, films, experiments, demonstrations, projects or planned experiences, assigned exercises, and testing of all kinds. The question of method, so regarded, is so large that its investigation requires subdivision, arbitrarily made for the sake of sharpness and coherence. Within four such divisions of the question of method we may raise the issues which, taken indiscriminately, have compounded the confusion of contemporary discussion.

First we can consider the methods—always including teaching techniques and apparatus—appropriate to the different stages of the whole educational process. The two easiest distinctions are those between adolescent schooling and adult learning and between the less and the more advanced phases of adolescent schooling. Is the education to be of the same kind at every stage or of different kinds? Should the differentiation, if any, be made in different schools or in the same school? Or should it be made outside of school and through other agencies or in adult education?

The second part of the inquiry is concerned with the adjustment of method, at whatever stage of education, to individual differences among the learners who are all at the same stage, for example, in elementary school or even in a given grade of elementary school. And here we are confronted with two separable questions: What should be done about individual differences in natural capacity for learning if such differences exist?

And what should be done about individual differences in interest, motivation, and future (or, in the case of adults, present) occupation?

The method of the preparation of teachers for a system of universal and compulsory schooling—and for adult education—is the third question, and it raises others: Are different methods of teacher-training indicated by the division of schooling into distinct stages? Is the teaching of adults so distinct from the teaching of adolescents that distinct methods are indicated for the preparation of adult educators? And if, since the learning process is never completed, adult education is a necessary stage of learning for all, how, if at all, should the training of the schoolteacher differ from that of the adult educator, and what kind of continuing adult education, if any, is appropriate to each of them?

The fourth problem of method is that of the advancement of learning. Although the dissemination and the advancement of learning are distinct functions, they are dynamically related. Not only the character and excellence of the technical means and apparatus but the very vitality of teaching depend upon the vigor of research. If in a particular educational system the university is the institution directly concerned with the advancement of learning, then this final question of method asks how the university is to be organized to advance learning most effectively.

These, then, are the most general categories into which the issues of education may be divided, at any time and in any fairly complex society. The consideration of education itself as a natural, artistic, and practical social enterprise asks the question, "What is education?" The consideration of objectives, institutions, and methods asks the questions, "What is it for?" and "How is it given?" The American revolution of 1850–1950 has produced a lot of labor-saving devices, but it has not produced a device for answering these questions.

CHAPTER 5

The American Focus

The democratic, industrial, and scientific conditions that have precipitated the educational crisis of our time themselves define some of the elements of the current controversy.

Democracy, for example, means universal suffrage, but universal suffrage is a travesty of democracy without free compulsory schooling for every child and equal educational opportunity in youth or in adult life. Industrialization means increased leisure and the economic possibility of extending free compulsory schooling far beyond the age of fourteen, but it also means increased mechanization and specialization of work and a consequent diminishing satisfaction of the instinct of workmanship. This means, in turn, two distinct new challenges to education—first, its relationship to increasingly mechanized occupations and, second, its relationship to the reduced satisfaction to be found in those occupations.

And a mature science and technology means not only a challenge to the validity or relevance of the thinking of pre-scientific history; it also means an ever accelerating tendency toward specialization in science and research. And this, in turn, means that education has got to decide whether preparation for specialization is its business, and to what extent, and at what level. In addition, science has, in one sense, enormously enlarged and, in another, enormously reduced the size of the individual's world, with cataclysmic consequences for the citizen's needed knowledge of geography, economics, politics, history, ethnology, language, literature, and even of theology and of science itself. Our immediate forebears did not have to know where Korea was, or the difference between Czechoslovakia and Yugoslavia; we have to know about Cambodia and Saudi Arabia and the difference between Vietnam and Vietminh.

The significance of our democratic, industrial, and technological development is lost if it is thought to rest entirely in an increased number of children in school for an increased number of years; and the present preoccupation, in the question of federal aid, with the shortage of classrooms and teachers indicates that the educational significance of the second American revolution is indeed lost. The mere increase in itself raises only the questions—no small questions, to be sure—of the cost of the system and the finding and training of an adequate number of competent teachers. But a much more serious problem arises when the number of children in school becomes the whole child population. The schoolroom at every level then includes the whole range of human differences in capacity, from a minimum of educability to the highest native endowment, and, in addition, the whole range of human differences in background, interest, motivation, and future occupation.

At first glance it would seem that this last problem is neither new nor peculiar. The educational system of every age has been confronted with such differences. But it met them only at the level of the elite, where, for the most part, the individual child was given individual attention if he needed it. Except for a few poor boys (self-selected as regards high native endowment), the learner's interest, motivation, and future occupation, in so far as they provided direction for his education, were fairly well defined, and his background completely so. He was going to be a member of the ruling and/or professional castes, as his ancestors were before him. If a second or third (or first) son was peculiarly ungifted, or overgifted, or misgifted, a place could be found for him somewhere in the privileged order where he could not do any harm.

Universal compulsory education in a uniquely heterogeneous population poses the problem of range in a very different way. It must deal not with a relatively few individuals but with whole categories of children of differing endowments and interests and levels of interest; with children of common workers natively competent to enter highly specialized or learned vocations; with children of the learned who are destined by endowment to enter common occupations; with interested and uninterested children and with interests as wide as the world; in a word, with a boundless range of prospective adulthood in which, whatever his occupation, every normal adult is going to be a free man and a sovereign citizen.

Modern American life raises, finally, a new educational question of almost incalculable magnitude. If every child is to be given adequate schooling, if every present or future citizen is to have equal educational opportunity, and if every worker is to have a life of substantial leisure, our society stands face to face with an issue which, up to now, has been met in haphazard fashion. It is the issue of adult education. And it is focused even more sharply by the answer we give to one of the questions raised in the general consideration of the nature of education itself: Is the goal of education—pursued by both nature and art —attainable in childhood and adolescence; or is it never achieved, in the sense that no one, no matter how much he has learned in a lifetime, has exhausted his natural capacity for learning?

If our answer is "No" to the first part of the question and "Yes" to the second, the requirement of nature that learning be carried on through life becomes in an industrial democracy a possibility to art and practice. As we observed earlier, the remedial night school of the turn of the century has all but disappeared with the cessation of large-scale immigration and with the spread of free compulsory education and its extension through high school. And the night school was not, in fact, adult education but, rather, adolescent education given to adults who had missed it. With some modifications it was a replica of the day schooling of children, and so was the immigrant orientation class.

But in a society which gives—or soon will give—all its children all the education they can profitably absorb, the education of adults takes on a character entirely its own. And here, as in the case of the school system, the agencies and programs of adult education must deal with the whole range of individual differences in capacity, background, interest, motivation, and occupation. The formal, public extension of adult education in the past half-century has been primarily vocational or specialized. But a rapidly increasing number of programs—sometimes in colleges and universities, sometimes in private organizations motivated by either special or public interest, and sometimes in public libraries in co-operation with private organizations—have arisen in all the fields of general education, concerned with social or personal problems, with cultural subjects, or with the arts. If we decide that the American situation implies universal (or at least universally available) adult education, we have to gird ourselves to consider objectives, institutional means, and methods in a sphere marked "undiscovered"—or at least "unexplored"—on the educational map.

CHAPTER 6

Bill of Particulars

When an author has to apologize for what he is going to say, he might save his own face (and the reader's annoyance) by refraining from saying it. The authors of this book have to apologize for this chapter and justify its inclusion. It is not incomprehensible; it is simply unreadable. It is a map of the areas in which the parts of the educational controversy lie, and, like any other map, it is meant to be studied, not read. Like any other map, too, it becomes more intelligible as the traveler becomes more familiar with the terrain. It attempts, in abstract, summary form, and as tersely as possible, to trace the outlines of the present discussion. The authors wrote it in the course of writing this book; the reader may find it similarly useful to read it in the course of reading the book, turning back to it to answer the question that led the authors to write it: "How did we get from *there* to *here?*" At this point, no more than a cursory reading need be given the statement of the subordinate issues enumerated *First, Second, Third*, etc.

THE ENDS OF EDUCATION

"The end of action," said an ancient Greek, "is its first principle." Until we know where we are going, there is not much point in starting to go there. So, in American education in the middle of the twentieth century, the first question is, "What are we trying to do?" To the extent and only to the extent that we can make progress in answering this question can we make meaningful progress in the other two great areas of the educational problem—the institutional means to be established and the methods to be employed. These are both means, however important in themselves, to the achievement of the ends we discover.

What, then, are the ends or objectives of education in an industrial democracy in an age of science? In the course of trying to answer this question, we find ourselves raising two other questions and several issues subordinate to each. The first: *Are the ends of education the same for all men regardless of individual differences?* This question involves two readily distinguishable issues:

> *First*—between those who maintain that the ends of education are the same for all and those who deny that they are.
>
> *Second*—between those who maintain that they are the same for all under all conditions of society and those who maintain that, while they are the same for all under conditions of a given society (ours, for example), they are different for societies in differing conditions (for example, in a primitive civilization or an undemocratic state).

The second of the two major questons raised by the consideration of objectives is this: *What kinds of education are there?* And here there are four readily distinguishable issues:

First—whether kinds of education can be distinguished; and, if so, whether the distinction can be made entirely in terms of objectives or also requires the consideration of institutions and methods.

Second—whether physical, moral, intellectual, and religious education are distinct, one from another, and especially whether moral and intellectual education can be separated.

Third—whether general and specialized education are to be distinguished, and, if so, how.

Fourth—whether liberal and vocational education are distinct, and, if so, how; and the relation of this distinction to that between general and specialized education.

THE INSTITUTIONS OF EDUCATION

When we turn to the consideration of the institutional agencies of education we find, again, two central questions and several issues raised by each of them. The first question is: *Can the school system achieve the objectives of education in childhood and in adolescence, or is further education necessary in adult life?* Here there are three subordinate issues:

First—between those who think that the education of adults is necessary even for those who have had considerable schooling in youth and those who think that it is not necessary.

Second—what kind or kinds of learning should adults acquire (among those who affirm the necessity of adult education)?

Third—between those who think that the education of youth, in objective, kind, quantity, and method, should be unaffected by the consideration of adult education and those who think that a scheme of adult education ought to affect the prior schooling of youth in any or all of these respects.

Underlying the whole question of adult education and the issues it raises is a complex of political and social problems. In no free society—or doctrine of free society—has it ever been advocated that adult education be compulsory. John Stuart Mill proposed an election procedure which would give more weight to the elector of superior intelligence, and this procedure, nowhere adopted, might be taken to constitute a strong inducement to adult education and to its public maintenance, but not to compulsion. Denmark's famous folk-high-school program is subsidized by the state, but, while young adults are urged to enter, it remains voluntary, as does adult education everywhere else (except for army indoctrination and specialized instruction). Even in totalitarian states, although great pressure may be put upon the people to participate in one kind of educational or indoctrination program or another, it is not compulsory upon all adults.

The adult has non-educational responsibilities and interests which are prior to his continuing education. Together with the cornerstone issue of individual liberty of choice, this fact raises questions as to the quantity and duration of adult education, its demands on the participant's time, the requirements (if any) for admission and continuance, the division into levels, the auspices under which it is conducted, the means by which participation is encouraged, etc. However these questions are answered—we shall come back to them later—this much appears to be clear: while formal learning is the center of childhood and adolescent life (however ardently the child himself may assert other responsibilities or interests or his right to individual liberty), it is secondary in adulthood.

The second major question raised by the consideration of the institutional agencies of education is: *What kind (or kinds) and amount of schooling should be given at different institutional stages?* And this question raises six obvious issues:

> *First*—between those who think that the same kind of education should be given to all during the whole period of

compulsory schooling and those who think that there should be an institutional stage at which different kinds of education are introduced (for example, liberal for some, vocational for others).

Second—what kind of education should be given to all (among those who think that there should be no differentiation)? Should it, for example, be liberal or vocational or both? Concerned with competence in reading, writing, and arithmetic, or with the development of right social attitudes and habits, or with the development of an integrated personality? And if any combination of these or other talents, what is the relative role of each?

Third—what should be school-leaving age, and, consequently, what should be the division of compulsory schooling into different institutional stages (and the duration of each)?

Fourth—what is the place of the college in the school system, and, especially, does any part of it belong to the system of free education for all, compulsory or not (for example, the junior college)?

Fifth—what kind of education should be offered at the college level (for example, general or specialized or both; vocational or liberal or both; and, if both, in what relationship)?

Sixth—between those who think that the school should concentrate on the development of the intellect and leave the other aspects of the child's development to other institutions in society and those who think that the school should concern itself with the whole development of the child.

THE METHODS OF EDUCATION

When, finally, we consider the methods of education (including the preparation of teachers), we find ourselves with five major questions, each of them raising one or more issues. The first question is: *Should individual differences among children affect the method of giving the same kind of basic education to all of them?* This question raises two issues:

> *First*—between those who think that individual differences can be met by different methods of teaching the same content and those who think that the content, as well as the method, must be differentiated.
>
> *Second*—between those who think that the same kind of education for all requires an entirely prescribed course of study and those who think that it permits electives at some point.

These same two issues recur at the college level, altered somewhat by the fact that college is at present voluntary and enrols only some of the adolescents who have completed compulsory basic schooling. Those who think that the upper level of college should offer specialized education are not concerned with the second issue, since specialized study calls for electives. The issue concerning electives is not simply whether they are appropriate in general education as opposed to specialized education but also whether the fact of individual differences among students, taken with the fact of their common humanity, does or does not require a curriculum combining elective with prescribed studies.

The second major question of method is closely related to the first: *What is the best method or combination of methods of giving the same kind of education at any given stage of schooling?* The many-sided issue raised by this question is that of the effectiveness of various techniques—books and reading, direct experience, experimentation, lectures, discussion, different types of testing, films, etc.—as both content and apparatus for achieving a single objective or set of objectives for education.

Next: *How are teachers to be trained?* And there are two basic issues here:

> *First*—between those who think that teachers can be adequately prepared by technical or vocational training at the end of their basic schooling and those who think that technical or vocational training should be postponed until after liberal education at the college level.

> *Second*—between those who think that teachers peculiarly need to continue postschool learning and those who think that they need it neither more nor less than other adults.

The fourth major issue of method is raised by the third: *How are teachers to be prepared for adult education?* This question is complicated by all the factors of adult life that affect the participation of mature, basically schooled persons in an educational program which ideally would continue through their lives. At the level of method, however, the preparation of the adult educator suggests three issues:

> *First*—the role of the adult educator and whether (and how) it differs from that of the schoolteacher.

> *Second*—the character of the adult learner and whether (and how) he differs from the juvenile learner.

> *Third*—depending on the resolution of the first and second issues, the content and method which the adult educator is to be prepared to administer.

The last question raised by the consideration of method is this: *How can the profession of teaching be assisted and improved by the advancement of learning?* Here there is one general issue as to method and one as to institution:

> *First*—between those who think that the advancement of learning through specialized study and research is enough and those who think that the improvement of general edu-

cation requires the advancement of learning as a whole through the interconnection of all fields of advanced study.

Second—between those who think that the departmentalized university is adequate to assist and improve the profession of teaching and those who think that the university would have to be partly or wholly reorganized on nondepartmental lines to do the job or that some other kind of institution must be established to do it.

All the particular issues enumerated in this chapter cannot be dealt with in this study or need they be, nor, indeed, for the purposes of this study, should they be. Our purpose is not to attempt to solve the particular problems of education but to discover and clarify, if possible, the ultimate issues underlying them, in the hope that they can be attacked with greater coherence.

Many of the issues just enumerated could be presented in different terms or in different contexts. Many of them are related as parts of one or another larger subject of dispute. Many involve questions of policy in the application of principles to particular circumstances. And many are subjects of dispute only at the level at which particular decisions have to be made. Finally, some of them can be resolved only by educational research or experiment, or at least against a background of further research and experiment than has up to now been conducted.

It is the issues involving conflict on the level of principles—practical principles, since we are dealing not with a pure science but with a social enterprise—that belong pre-eminently to the philosophy of education itself. And it is in the philosophy of education that we are certain to find the ultimate controversies that sometimes fail to emerge, or, emerging, fail to be recognized, in the arena of educational debate.

CHAPTER 7

Principle, Policy, and Practice

Opening the White House Conference on Education in 1955, President Killian of the Massachusetts Institute of Technology said:

It is obviously vital for this Conference to open with an examination of goals. We cannot proceed in any orderly way to build, staff, and finance a school until we agree on the job we want the school to do. Many misunderstandings can be cleared up before more immediate "practical" problems are considered. Too often school problems are discussed backwards—beginning with demanding day-to-day matters and working back slowly—and perhaps never getting to fundamental principles. People who disagree on the fundamental principles cannot easily agree on school budgets, or on much of anything else connected with education.

The funny thing is that they do. Under the pressure or, rather, the combination of conflicting pressures that beat upon the schools, people who disagree on fundamental principles simply ignore both their disagreement and their fundamental principles and get on with the job. President Killian ought to be right; it ought to be impossible for people who disagree fundamentally to work together. But since they must work together, and since they have no time to discuss fundamentals, and since they would find themselves inevitably challenging one or another of the conflicting pressures upon them if they did, they work together superficially. The schools and the school systems *do* operate somehow.

"What characterizes American education," says one of America's most experienced educators, Director Ralph W. Tyler of the Center for Advanced Study in the Behavioral Sciences, "is not a bad philosophy, but no philosophy." The reasons are not far to find. We are still a young people, nationally, immensely heterogeneous in background, and preoccupied from our very beginning (not so long ago) with an unparalleled material expansion. Under such conditions it is no surprise that we are not notably philosophical. And what is true for the country as a whole is even more emphatically true for education. We have been head over heels building schools, finding teachers, and putting children into seats (and keeping them there). The mind of man runs to the immediate, in any case, and our schools have had to go just as fast as they can to keep up with it.

Nor should we underestimate the insight of democracy's greatest student, De Tocqueville, who warned a century ago that private life in successful and equalitarian societies "is so busy, so excited, so full of wishes and of work, that hardly any energy or leisure remains to each individual for public life. . . . The love of public tranquility is frequently the only passion which these nations retain, and it becomes more active and powerful amongst them in proportion as all other passions droop and die." Even if we do not recognize ourselves with

complete clarity in this portrait, we may still concede its validity in our usually widespread contentment with our public
institutions as long as they let us alone and (until very recently) with our schools as long as they are conveniently located and adequately heated in winter. Educational philosophy
could be left to the teachers.

But the teachers (and administrators) have been too sorely
tried by the problems of the moment and too wildly buffeted
by private and public interest groups with conflicting demands
on the curriculum to meditate fundamentals or, indeed, to
meditate at all. The here and the now have been obsessive, and
those few Americans who have made it a practice to attend
meetings of their local school boards can testify uniformly to
the difficulty these public servants have in merely keeping the
system from falling or bursting or being pulled or pushed apart.

True, philosophy of education is meaningless if it is detached
from the circumstances of time and place, because education is
first and last a practical enterprise, constructed each day under
changing conditions of community life, conditions which are
never exactly the same in any two places or at any two times.
The principles of a philosophy of education must be practical
principles, by which practical policies and particular practices
can be directed and judged. But in any practical enterprise
there are levels of thinking, three in number, that can be distinguished without too much effort.

The law, the oldest and best settled such enterprise, provides
us with the most clearly defined example. Closest to action—at
which all three levels of thinking aim—is the specific legal decision in a particular case here and now. The decision com-
mands that *this act* be performed. But the case is decided in
terms of a more general kind of thinking, the laws, and the
laws themselves are made on the basis of a still more general
kind of thinking, legal principles—at their simplest, such precepts as "Thou shalt not kill" or "Thou shalt not steal."

But even these principles, representing the third and highest level of legal thinking, derive from a level of thinking that is higher still. That is the level at which men think about what is good and bad, right and wrong, just and unjust, both for individuals and for societies. This last is higher than the three levels of legal thinking in the sense that it is broader than the principles, policies, and practices of the restricted sphere of law; it is concerned with the fundamental judgments which must be made in every practical enterprise, in business and education as well as in law. It belongs not to any of those special areas of thought but to moral and political philosophy.

So, in education, we have to think about specific decisions here and now (comparable to particular cases in law), about policies of school systems (comparable to laws themselves), and about principles of education (comparable to the legal precepts from which laws are derived). But (as in law) there is a higher level than that of the principles of the art itself—the level, again, on which we ask what is good and bad for the individual and for society. It is the level of philosophy, and even those who, in any vocation, think that their principles are contained within the vocation itself, find themselves using as axioms philosophical judgments which they have taken for granted.

At the level of educational decision, one state may, for example, decide that public schooling should begin at the age of six, another at the age of five; both decisions arise under the accepted educational policy of compulsory schooling, which, in turn, is the implementation of the educational principle of equal opportunity. Accepting the principle of equal opportunity, two educators may differ regarding the policy of the duration of compulsory schooling. And they may disagree at the level of principle, interpreting equal opportunity differently, one of them holding that differentiated, the other that undifferentiated, schooling serves it. Or they may disagree about democracy, one of them maintaining the principle of equal opportunity, the other rejecting it; and here their quarrel has transcended education and entered political philosophy. For it is in political philosophy, and not in the philosophy of education, that the principle of equal educational opportunity seeks its validity.

The bitterest kind of conflict may be engendered between two educators who, without knowing it, are making judgments on different levels. They may appear to be in conflict when in reality they are not. They cannot resolve the conflict because they are talking (and may go on doing so for years, "slugging it out") about two different things. When one party to an educational debate is defending a policy and the other a principle—and that fact is known to them both—the first may well accept the principle and the second find an alternative policy acceptable to the first under that principle.

Does this sound like so much juggling of words? Just consider one of the hottest subjects of educational debate, the so-called whole-child controversy. One educator holds that the schools should concern themselves primarily with intellectual discipline, leaving the major emphasis on other aspects of human development to other agencies; another holds that the schools should concern themselves with every aspect of human development and with some aspects (such as physical or emotional adjustment or vocational preparation) as much as with the intellect. If they were to discover that on principle they are allies, not enemies, that they both accepted the principle that education is indeed the development of the "whole child," and that their argument is over the efficacy of alternative policies directed toward that development, they might have a chance of reaching agreement—a better chance, at least, than they have when they think that they are divided on fundamental principle.

Since educational judgments made at any level—of principle, policy, or particular practice—are practical judgments involving the merits of alternative actions, they necessarily depend in part upon knowledge or opinion about matters of fact. But only in part. Facts are descriptive. They tell us what is the case, in particular or generally; they do not tell us what to do about it. But educational judgments are, in the end, not descriptive but prescriptive. They tell us what to do. They direct a course of action.

It is precisely at this point, where a judgment must be made as to what to do educationally, that the still more fundamental principles, the principles upon which judgments are made about good and bad, right and wrong, just and unjust, come into play. And these are "normative" or "moral" or "value" judgments, indicating what should or should not be done in a given situation, with due regard to all the facts involved. Educational controversy, at least at the level of principle (and often at that of policy), is likely to be concerned with these ultimate judgments of value, and, unless the controversialists see that it is so concerned, they may proceed in a circle for as long as good manners sustain them—and then, neither of them having seen where the issue actually lay, they may abandon each other as incurably stupid or, no less commonly, as incurably bigoted.

To be sure, questions of fact are of the utmost importance in the discussion of educational issues at every level. What is more, they are relevant, and fundamentally relevant, to the ultimate questions of value underlying the conflict of educational principles; whether a man should be punished lightly or heavily or at all for stealing a loaf of bread or killing a fellow man is in part determined by the fact that he was or was not starving or insane at the time he did the deed. Our lives and societies are centered in the world of fact; our perceptions, our learning, and, consequently, our judgments begin with fact. To say what ought to be or what ought to be done without discovering what is, is meaningless.

But the way in which questions of fact are relevant to educational debate differs at the different levels of principle, policy, and particular practice, and here again the field of law, in which the delineation is exceptionally clear, provides a familiar parallel. In the decision of a particular case at law, the application of the statute to the case depends upon a judgment of the *particular* facts of the case. At the level of legislation (or policy-making) the formulation of the statute depends upon *generally* prevalent facts. And at the level of legal principles, to which statutes are conformed, both the principles and the ultimate judgments of value from which they derive rest upon *universal* facts about the nature of man, about human relations, and about the organization of society.

In the field of education the role of facts is very much the same. Policy is never determined by the particular case. Given, for instance, the principle of a completed basic education for every child, experimentation may be necessary to determine whether basic education can be better achieved by a 6–4–4 program ending at age twenty, by a 6–3–3 program ending at eighteen, by an 8–4–4 program ending at twenty-two, or by some other division and terminal point. In addition to general experimentation and measurement, the history of education may contribute facts (or at least clues of a descriptive character) that are relevant to the formulation of the policy. But little Johnny Jones of 1423 Lincoln Street may complete his basic education at fourteen or at twenty-four or never and in one stage of schooling or in three or in six; in his particular case, exception to the policy is obviously called for.

Above the level of policy, the issues of educational principle (and the ultimate judgments of value from which the principles derive) are determined by the hardest of all facts to find— the universal facts about the nature of man and society and about the nature of the human mind, of experience, of knowledge, and of learning and teaching. Questions of this order cannot be answered by educational research, just as ultimate legal principles cannot be determined, and never are, by the infinite collection of legal rules established under conditions which, while they are not, on the one hand, particular, are not, on the other, universal. Whether or not man has free will is not determined either by *this man's* behavior or by *this society's*.

True, the empirical social sciences gather the raw materials, classify them, and present them. But the answers—at least to the most fundamental questions—lie in that most difficult and controversial of all fields, philosophy. It has been said that "the queen of the sciences" is like a woman—impossible to live with, impossible to live without. Men who are unwilling to make settled and explicit philosophical judgments because they expect some particular or general fact to come along and contradict the universal which philosophy asserts nevertheless live by such judgments in their every volitional act. They cannot escape behaving as if there were such universals, whether or not there are; they cannot begin each day, when they meet a man on the street, with a mind that is blank as to the nature of man.

Educational theory centers around the principles of education and therefore moves in the direction of the moral or political judgments on which the principles rest. Discussion of educational theory tends also to include the more general policies to which the principles give rise. Educational practice, on the other hand, flows immediately from the policies of a particular society. But the policies, while they lead to decisions about actions in particular cases, also lead back to the principles from which they emanate.

This study is trying to examine the educational controversy in America today on the plane of theory. Since educational theory is practical even as theory (in that its principles concern action and govern policies and decisions), we may not be able to ignore certain very general questions of policy closely connected with disputes about the educational principles appropriate to an industrialized democracy in an age of science. But where policy moves in the direction of detail and of particular decisions, it is neither possible nor profitable to encompass it in this discussion; impossible because of the immensity of variation from school system to school system, from school to school within a given system, and even within a given school; unprofitable because the decision so often depends upon matters of fact which can be ascertained only by educational research or experiment.

The great disputes in educational theory go beyond education to questions of moral and political thought—and beyond them to ultimate issues in science and philosophy and the relationship of the two. The commonly accepted divisions of education—the school system, adult education, the teaching profession, and the advancement of learning—will serve for our examination of the controversy itself. But we shall have to proceed from there to a confrontation of the philosophical issues on which the controversy finally rests, culminating in the relationship of philosophy and science. This is, by all odds, the greatest issue of all and is rarely argued—or even recognized—outside the small circle of professional philosophers. We must argue it here if we are going to discharge our obligation to go to the bottom of the controversy in American education.

PART III

The Issues

CHAPTER 8

No Uncertain Terms

Educators are sometimes, like boxers, pugnacious. But there the similarity ends. The boxer studies his opponent's position and makes sure that he understands it. He knows that, if he misinterprets it or ignores it, he is lost the minute he steps into the ring. The educator does not step into the ring with his opponent. He publishes a paper—or delivers a speech—in one journal—or hall—and his opponent in another. In the course of his solo performance he ascribes to his opponent a position which his opponent immediately denies holding. So the two parties, unlike boxers, never meet.

Nor will they as long as Jones, who is for democracy (or liberty, or growth, or development, or whatever), insists that Smith, who disagrees with him on education, is against democracy (or liberty, or whatever). The fact is that Jones and

Smith are opponents in some respects and components in others and that educational issues, like other issues, cannot be resolved (or even stated) in pot-and-kettle terms. Wherever there are real issues, there are real oppositions, but the oppositions reside, in their pristine purity, only in the issues and not in the antagonists. If the antagonists would try to reduce the issues to irreducibles, they might have occasion to discover that they agreed where they thought they disagreed—and disagreed where they thought they agreed.

The ultimate reduction of issues is to terms. In this analysis of the issues in education, six terms emerge from the ultimate reduction. These, in pairs, are "aristocrat" and "democrat," "realist" and "idealist," and "traditionalist" and "modernist." Now there are two difficulties in using terms. One is that they simplify, and simplification verges always on oversimplification. The other is that they sometimes sound like epithets. Jones, who admits being a realist (and is proud of it), denies that he has no ideals; and Smith, while he claims to be an idealist, will not for a moment concede that Jones has a monopoly on realism. They are both right, doubtless, and both of them are justifiably aggrieved at being strait-jacketed. Each in fact shares the other's position at this point or that and to some degree. It might be more useful—if less dramatic—to talk about positions instead of persons.

True, the disadvantage of oversimplification persists, even when we talk about positions instead of persons. But this disadvantage is inescapable whenever the effort is made to reduce issues to irreducible terms. If the parties to the discussion are aware of the disadvantage and are willing to tolerate it for the sake, not of the arguer, but of the argument, there is a possibility that they will find it less disadvantageous than the alternatives of epithet-hurling, commencement oratory, or politely vague palaver. There is nothing wrong with straw men, provided they are recognized for what they are at the outset.

Like puppets, they can serve an edifying purpose, and, again like puppets, they can fight to the finish without losing their tempers.

We shall attempt, therefore, to discover the basic issues in American education by resorting to calling names—not of persons but of positions. The disclaimer must at once be entered that any resemblance to any person living or dead is not only coincidental but impossible. None of these positions is personified in any existing individual; Jones, who holds a whole complex of vews, is an "aristocrat" in one respect, a "democrat" in another. Nor do any of these terms have anything specific to do with commonplace images. The "aristocrat" of our analysis is not a landowner who lashes his peasants; the "democrat" does not throw his arms around his neighbor in the streetcar. The "idealist" is not a poet who forgets to tie his shoelaces; the "realist" does not foreclose the widow's mortgage; the "traditionalist" does not drive a horse and buggy; and the "modernist" is not a "be-bop" fan in a Hollywood sports shirt.

These non-existent characters, "constructs," as the logician would call them, weave in and out of our analysis, paired, unpaired, and variously paired again. Jones and Smith will not find themselves opposed here; they will not find themselves at all. But it is hoped that they will find, each of them, all of the parts of their educational thinking here; that the parts, always designated and always in the same way, will be distinguishable throughout; and that neither Jones nor Smith, although both of them may say that the authors' reasoning is fallacious, will be moved to say, "I don't know what he's talking about."

For the purpose of discourse the three pairs of positions—"aristocrat" and "democrat," "realist" and "idealist," and "traditionalist" and "modernist"—move across the stage of this analysis as if they were embodied. But only for the purpose of discourse. When we say, "The realist holds" or "The traditionalist replies," we mean that the realist position holds or that the traditionalist position replies. We beseech the reader to depersonalize these six terms and, if he finds any of them "loaded," either with infamy or with splendor, to "de-load" them. On the whole, he could proceed just as fruitfully (if somewhat more cumbersomely) by calling them "A" and "B," "C" and "D" and "E" and "F" throughout.

The issues themselves, in which these six positions take form, arise in connection with the school system—that is, with the principles, policies, and practices involved in the education of adolescents through high school and, for a growing minority of their number, through college. It is at this level that the issues are commonly defined and commonly joined. They reappear, however, at the other two levels of education, namely, adult education and professional study, involving not only the advancement of learning but also the preparation of teachers. After attempting to locate the issues in the school system, we shall consider them at the other two levels, both in their own terms and in relation to the school system.

CHAPTER 9

The Aristocrat and the Democrat

Six conditions of modern American life underlie the controversy in education. They are:

1. The extension of the franchise toward universal suffrage.

2. The extension of universal free compulsory education from six or eight to ten or twelve years.

3. The extension of universal free education beyond the compulsory period for a rapidly growing proportion of the rising generation in public junior colleges and colleges.

4. The extension of industrial production and organization, with its attendant consequences of increased division of labor, shortening of the work week, and the abolition (or attenuation) of the distinction between a leisure class and a laboring class.

5. The development of the thesis that democracy requires equal educational opportunity for all.

6. The development of the thesis of human equality, in the light of individual differences or inequalities with respect to native capacities and talents, social and economic background, and, in the case

of children, the educational opportunities and attainments of their parents.

It will be seen at once that these six conditions of modern American life lie outside the field of education. Although their consequences for education are fundamental and decisive, they have got to be discussed in terms not of educational philosophy but of moral and political philosophy and even of theology. They distinguish the aristocratic from the democratic view as a whole, and not just as regards educational principles. The other two pairs of positions (idealist and realist and traditionalist and modernist) represent essentially educational views. But these views cannot be argued until the conclusions of the aristocratic-democratic controversy are reached, because those conclusions are the principles from which the arguments of the other four positions all take their departure.

One further observation about these six conditions: together they reflect the democratic and industrial revolution of the United States in the past century. The third element of this revolution, namely, the transition from a pre-scientific to a scientific and technological culture, related as it is to both the democratic and the industrial development, has nevertheless had such singular consequences for the controversy in education that it is reserved for separate analysis and discussion in Part V of this book.

The ancient aristocrat (who, of course, is not a party to the present controversy) ignores the first five conditions of modern American life because he denies the sixth. He denies the natural equality of men and justifies the institution of slavery (in one form or another) in terms of natural inequality. Distinguishing free men by nature from slaves by nature, he distinguishes education from training. Education, liberal in purpose and character, is for free men, for citizenship, leisure, and lofty pursuits. Slaves, serfs, manual workers, and even skilled artisans are trained, much as animals are trained. They are given whatever training or apprenticeship they need to master their specific functions of production or service, and no more. The notion, for example, that a woodworker, however highly skilled, should study poetry or music would never occur to our ancient aristocrat.

Aristotle held that some men are by nature slaves, on the ground that they have only enough reason to follow directions given by others but not enough to direct their own lives. They lack a "deliberative faculty." Yet, because they are able to participate in reason passively, they also differ from animals, who are driven by their instincts. The natural slave is, therefore, a man, not a brute, and yet as a human being he is inferior to the man who is by nature free. This, says Aristotle, is a "difference of kind, not of degree"—a difference which justifies the use of the natural slave as an instrument in the service of his master. "The use made of slaves and of tame animals," Aristotle writes, "is not very different; for both with their bodies minister to the needs of life." To whatever degree beyond animal training the slave's "education" might be carried, it is clear that its controlling purpose was the master's good, not the slave's.

A division did exist among the ancient aristocrats analogous to the division we shall encounter later among modern realists. Some, like Aristotle, attempted to justify the existing institution of slavery on the ground that at least the enslavement of those who were by nature intended to be slaves is "both expedient and right." Others, by far the majority, simply accepted the institution (or, rather, its economic and social benefits to themselves) without any thought about its basis. The practice of enslavement by war mocked the doctrine of natural slavery, for free Greek enslaved free Greek and not just the barbarian, who was assumed to be an inferior kind of man. Aristotle condemned such enslavement as contrary to nature and unjust; and, in addition, he was compelled to admit that among his contemporaries there were some who maintained that "the distinction between slave and freeman exists by law only, and not by nature; and being an interference with nature is therefore unjust." But, for the most part, an incurious acceptance of the existing order characterized the society as a whole, in ancient Athens as in old Alabama.

Like his ideological ancestor, the modern aristocrat denies—or ignores as educationally irrelevant—the first five conditions of American life listed above. But he differs from the ancients in that he accepts the sixth. All men are equal as persons, and this equality invalidates the institution of slavery. But, says the modern aristocrat, the unequal natural abilities among equal persons do distinguish the educable from the ineducable or the highly educable from the less educable. This position is not so fatuous as it sounds in George Orwell's satire of the totalitarian "democracy" in which "all men are equal, but some are more equal than others." Rejecting slavery as firmly as the democrat does, the modern aristocrat argues that only a minority are capable of absorbing an education that is liberal in character and purpose. Universal public schooling should be reduced to the minimum required for the exigencies of common life; beyond that point the majority, incapable of liberal education, should be trained for specific economic tasks.

That the aristocratic position is unpopular does not take it out of court. The modern political "liberal," when he asserts his abhorrence of it, is generally unaware that his hero Jefferson at least in some measure embraced it. It is earnestly advanced by men who are not unintelligent, dishonest, or even necessarily antagonistic to political and economic democracy. And as we shall see when we discuss the realist position (and especially when we talk of vocational education), the position is widely held in our own educational system and still more widely in those areas of Europe whence our democratic institutions sprang.

One extremely important qualification has to be made re-

garding the modern aristocrat. When he talks about educability, he is talking about the educability of the individual. He
would in no case consider any category of human beings—national, occupational, racial—more or less educable than any
other or make an educational distinction on any other basis
than individual endowment. And when he talks about educability, he is talking only about individual endowment and is
perfectly willing to admit that the appearance of ineducability
may, in some individual cases, be the consequence of inept
method. If he has had any experience at all of teaching, he
knows of instances in which "hopeless" students have proved,
under greater or more appropriate stimulation than they were
getting, to be good and even brilliant.

What he is talking about is *nature* and the natural capacity
of the individual under the best possible auspices. The optimistic view that all children are natively competent to absorb and
use a liberal education nourished the rise of democracy, but the
experience of democracy has not yet resolved the issue indisputably in favor of optimism. Throughout modern discussion
the question has been raised—sometimes inadvertently—by men
whose dedication to democracy is beyond cavil. More than
fifty years ago John Dewey said that "the simple facts of the
case are that in the great majority of human beings the distinctively intellectual interest is not dominant. They have the so-
called practical impulse and disposition." A quarter-century
later Bertrand Russell thought it possible that "there would not
be much independence of thought even if education did everything to promote it," and at about the same time Alfred North
Whitehead, in *The Aims of Education*, expected, he said, that
"artisan children will want something more concrete and, in
a sense, swifter than [the liberal curriculum] I have set down
here."

While all these observations would, in fairness, require a more
careful exegesis than can be made here, all of them seem to be-

tray a degree of uncertainty, however nebulous, on the point of actual educability. Nor have the more recent developments in our school situation alleviated that uncertainty. No less distinguished an idealistic democrat than Bernard Iddings Bell, in his recent *Crisis in Education*, after saying that a liberal education "would have lifted [the Common Man] into the stature of the Free Man, the Citizen Man, the Liberal Man. It would have bestowed on him an intellectual and spiritual emancipation comparable to his economic emancipation," proceeds to an apparent contradiction of this optimistic view in a statement so pessimistic as to be positively grim:

> Most students now in college can never be made into persons competent to lead anyone, even themselves. Not only are they in residence with other, lesser ends in view, but also most of them are not endowed with the kind of mind that may be developed to any great degree of discrimination. From birth their synaptic connections have been too slow for that. In the jargon of the moment, their IQ's (intelligence quotients) are too low. They share the more pedestrian lot of most of God's children. They are human beings and as such are of infinite worth, beloved of the Deity and to be loved by the brethren, but their *chief* activity is bound to be the hewing of wood and drawing of water and tending of machines.

This does not mean that Canon Bell, any more than John Dewey or Bertrand Russell, is one with the ancient aristocrat who divided men categorically into free and slave or educable and ineducable. He would have every child liberally taught "to the full extent of what facility he or she may have." And "the few who are potentially intelligent . . . may come from rich parents or poor, from slum homes or from palaces." It does mean that the question of the extent of *born* educability is still moot in respectable quarters.

The president of the University of Virginia recently recommended that compulsory public education beyond grammar school should be abandoned. He urged the return, he said, to Jefferson's view that "we are obligated to teach every child to read and write. . . . After that, it is our obligation, as Jefferson visualized it, to provide a really fine education beyond reading and writing for the students who show talent and interest." Albert Jay Nock, citing Jefferson's proposal as "the severest possible judgment against the popular perversion which we have followed ever since his day," goes much further than President Darden. Accepting what he calls "the philosophical doctrine of equality," which nullifies slavery, Nock denies that the doctrine requires political equality.

Nock's view, more extreme than that of John Stuart Mill, with his ballot weighted on the basis of intelligence, nevertheless recalls us to the fact that the great Victorian advocate of human liberty had reservations about across-the-board egalitarianism. It is, says Nock, a fundamental error to suppose that democracy is "a matter of the extension of the franchise" or "a matter of the individual's right to self-expression in politics." Democracy is purely economic, a matter of the diffusion of economic ownership and the right to own. We have, he says, to train "to the best advantage" a vast number of "ineducable persons." This, he thinks, our social system is pretty well organized to do. But our educational institutions "at present feel a certain responsibility, all the way through the system, over and above their function as training schools, for doing as much education as under their very untoward circumstances they are able to do. This is a great disability, and it should be removed."

Thus the aristocrat, accepting as he does the principle of human equality, insists that the principle be drastically qualified by the facts of individual inequality and that these qualifications have drastic educational consequences.

The democrat now emerges from the wings to take up the cause against the aristocrat. He accepts all six conditions of modern American life and accuses the aristocrat of taking supposition for fact as to educability. Without particular reference to the quality of college education, he takes note of the revelation provided by the Army General Classification Test in the last war that at least 49 per cent of the college-age population of the country has the ability to complete two years of college work. But natural inequality remains the strongest weapon in the aristocrat's arsenal, and the democratic position is plagued by this fact—or body of facts and/or suppositions—and its effect on the precept of equal educational opportunity.

Human equality calls for universal suffrage, say the democrats. Universal suffrage requires an educated—not merely a literate—citizenry. All men are educable, more educable than the aristocrat supposes. But how much more, and in what way? Here the democrats fall out among themselves, and for the same reason that all of them differ from the aristocrats—namely, because of the significance of the facts (or suppositions) of human inequalities among human equals.

CHAPTER 10

The Realist and the Idealist

The aristocrat—or, rather, the aristocratic position—now leaves the stage of the controversy. The democrat retires momentarily (and in some confusion) and re-enters from *both* wings. The plot is about to thicken. For here we have the democratic realist, and here the democratic idealist. Cheering is discountenanced, and favoritism frowned upon. The audience is once more reminded that the realist and the idealist are not isolated, undiluted personages; that neither one of them or the other is heroic or depraved; that both represent partial positions; that, in a word, and without celebration of the term "democratic," they may just as fairly be designated as Democrat A and Democrat B.

The heart of the issue between them is differentiation—the division of students into two or more groups at a certain stage of schooling, one group continuing in one kind of school, another in another; or (as is more common) all of them remaining in the same school but one group getting one kind of education, another another. The realist accepts or urges differentiation. The idealist thinks that it should be abolished from basic education altogether.

Since the idealist does not object to such differentiation after the whole period of basic schooling, his position is likely to be confused with that of the realist, or only vaguely distinguished from it. But the opposition between them is sharp. The realist accepts the system in which differentiation begins with secondary school (or at least with its last two years). The idealist would extend undifferentiated education to the very end of basic schooling, through two or even four years of college. Sharp as the opposition is between them at this point, it arises from an even sharper opposition, as we shall see.

There is some literal validity in using these two terms to describe these two positions. There really are differences in the kinds of education offered in the American school system today, and the realist maintains that these differences square with the real facts of human inequality. The idealist holds that only an undifferentiated school system is consistent with the democratic ideal and argues that the "facts" of human inequality are not real facts; there is, therefore, in his view, no factual basis for differentiation.

Now the argument is joined. The realist defends (or urges) differentiation. He may wish to reform American education in other fundamental respects, but in respect to differentiation he wishes only to improve its practice, the better to serve the ends of the individual and society. The idealist, on the contrary, regards all other reforms of education as subordinate to the abolition of differentiation.

However, neither party is hopelessly dogmatic. Among the realists, for example, there is general consensus that, for democ-

racy's sake, differentiation should be postponed as long as possible—although they do not agree among themselves how long
it can be postponed. In addition, for every realist who urges
differentiation on the basis of natural inequalities, there is one
who, without urging it, says that it has got to be accepted because of the existing inequalities of economic opportunity. In
the nature of things as they are, Tom has to go to work at
eighteen—or seventeen or sixteen—and be trained for a job
somewhere. If the high school will make a good airplane mechanic of him, he has an occupational advantage. On the other
hand, there is Harry, who at eighteen—or twenty—is wonder-
ing (though not too strenuously) what to do, but his parents
are well fixed, and, anyway, Harry likes to read and study.
And in between is Dick, who is determined to go into medicine
or the ministry if he has to beg, borrow, or steal to get there.

The idealist insists that differentiation can be avoided all the
way through college, in spite of natural inequalities and in spite
of Tom's vocational need. But he is likely to admit that his insistence is in part a matter of faith; until undifferentiated education is tried on a mass basis, we cannot be sure that it will
work. And for every idealist who thinks that differentiation
can be avoided by the discovery of different methods for giving
all children the same liberal education once given an elite, there
is one who thinks that the character of liberal education itself
must be altered if it is to be offered every child.

However they disagree among themselves—and however un-
sure of themselves they are in the absence of further experimentation—the idealists are as one in deploring the now prevalent and notorious dilution of the curriculum to the point
where Shakespeare, because he is "too hard" for the poorest
student, is read by none, or physics, because it is "too hard" for
the poorest student, is replaced by a "survey" course of the
sciences which touches each subject so superficially that nothing is learned that resembles scientific knowledge. This water-

ing-down of common education to its present low estate is usually justified by the realist on the basis of the requirement that the schools accept and keep—and, under crowded conditions, pass on to the next grade—every child. The custodial problem is so enormous that educational values have to be sacrificed. The children have to be kept in the school building, and kept there with minimum strain on an inadequate staff.

In the face of this numerical crisis the realist shrugs his shoulders and says that Shakespeare or physics is simply too hard for many pupils (or teachers). The idealist replies that anything that is badly taught, or taught under bad conditions, appears to be too hard, and he accuses the realist of defaming the learning ability of the young when he ought to be fighting for better conditions of teaching, better teachers, and better methods. The idealist knows that the student has to be interested in what he is supposed to learn if he is ever going to learn it, and he holds that the apparent disinterest of the apparently poor student—to whose level the whole system is lowered—is the consequence of poor teaching under stultifying conditions.

The fact, says the idealist, that some subjects are hard does not mean that they are necessarily uninteresting; "hard" is not the same thing as "too hard." Professor Arthur Bestor of the University of Illinois says that this adjustment of the curriculum always downward to the "slow learners"—jargon for dumbbells—will produce a whole generation of unlettered men and women. Bestor compares the downgrading of content to watering of the soup for extra dinner guests; everybody gets a plateful, but nobody is very well nourished. "Education," says Whitehead, "is the acquisition of the art of the utilization of knowledge. This is an art very difficult to impart. Whenever a text-book is written of real educational worth, you may be quite certain that some reviewer will say that it will be difficult to teach from it. Of course it will be difficult to teach from it. If it were easy, the book ought to be burned; for it cannot be educational." Former Chancellor Hutchins of the University of Chicago is fond of Aristotle's cryptic observation that "education is accompanied by pain."

The great area of differentiation that now exists in the American school system—and which the realist regards as at some point ineradicable—is the differentiation between liberal and vocational training. The point here is not at what age or grade level the differentiation occurs but what constitutes the difference in kinds of education. In content and in method there are many varieties of both liberal and vocational education. What distinguishes all of them as, on the one hand, essentially liberal and, on the other, essentially vocational is the aim or goal the varieties of each have in common.

Essentially—and the term is important—the aim of vocational education is the development of the individual's skill to undertake one or another kind of task in the economy, menial or exalted, and thereby to earn a living and perform a useful service in society. And the essential aim of all liberal education is to develop the individual's mind for the confrontation of the moral, political, and aesthetic problems of later life.

Neither kind of education entirely excludes the other in practice, or the other's aim. Any considerable skill involves aesthetics and can be involved with moral and political judgment. And liberal education, certainly indirectly and perhaps directly, equips a person for such vocations as statesmanship, journalism, and law. It would be hard to find in the American schools a program of liberal education that did not include, in principle and in practice, some instruction and operation in the useful or productive arts, and equally hard to find a program of vocational education that did not include some study of, say, literature or history. But the essential distinction in aim remains.

Both kinds of schooling may be said to look to later leisure (except for one extreme variety of vocational education, narrow and intensive job training—which is generally discredited even as vocational education, however widely it may be practiced). The vocationally well-educated man will use his learning in his spare time to develop his skills still further and even to contribute new methods or apparatus in his vocational field. His counterpart in liberal education will use his free time for the enjoyment and advancement of his own and of others' learning.

Differentiation of schooling, following a common core of learning, is to be argued primarily in relation to three aspects of human life—citizenship, labor, and leisure. The realist sees the child prepared for citizenship, for the common social responsibilities of every adult in a democracy, by the common core of learning before differentiation occurs and by such common elements of education as may be retained in the differentiated program. From the standpoint of future citizenship, then, he tends to advocate the longest possible postponement of differentiation and the greatest possible retention of the common elements of education after it occurs. He says, for example, that even after differentiation the vocational student should, if possible, study some English, perhaps history, literature, and a foreign language, along with general courses in those sciences related to his future vocation.

But the catch in the realist's position is the phrase "if possible." Labor, he says, to which all men are called, is generally of two distinct kinds: mechanical, technical, or managerial (of whatever grade or skill) and professional or intellectual (scientific, literary, artistic, etc.). Therefore, young people should be divided by vocational and liberal (or pre-professional) education, respectively. The highest skills or techniques require such intensive training that the realist, who would have them taught in school, finds himself with such a specialized curriculum that there is little or no place in it for non-vocational studies. As for the merchant—shopkeeper, salesman, clerk—or subprofessional "white-collar" worker, he requires very limited skill of a specialized character; his education can, therefore, be more heavily liberal than that of the skilled mechanical worker, but it is still essentially vocational in aim.

As for the employment of free time, says the realist, the less gifted or less fortunate child is prepared for its use both by the common elements of study (before and after his vocational studies begin) and by his developing interest in his vocation itself, while the more gifted or more fortunate child receives the additional benefits of liberal education. Here again the realist realistically shrugs his shoulders: One man enjoys an evening of Goethe or Bach and another of Elvis Presley or canasta —and who is to say which of the two is enjoying himself the more? Besides, they can both play golf without discrimination on the basis of their education, and, if the liberally educated man is more adept at discussion, the vocationally educated man is more adept at do-it-yourself operations.

In substantial agreement on differentiation, the realists are divided among themselves (as we have observed) in the way they look at it. One group, including a large proportion of American educators (and especially educational administrators), accepts differentiation as an inescapable reality arising, in part, perhaps, from natural inequalities, but in larger part from obvious social and economic inequalities. A second group, much smaller, holds that differentiation is called for by natural inequalities entirely apart from social and economic conditions and urges an improved system of differentiation rather than acquiescence in the haphazard patterns that now exist.

The second position is the clearer and more specific, inasmuch as it does not depend upon the kind of inequality society may be capable of removing. Professor Robert Ulich, for example, in maintaining the second position, argues that differences in intellectual capacity manifest themselves at about the twelfth year of life and can be discerned and measured by standard tests; that, therefore, after six years of common elementary learning, children should be divided into five groups according to the future type of labor indicated by their natural capacities—humanists, scientists, executives, artisans, and common workers. He would have the secondary-school program reconstructed according to these five groupings, although he would retain in all five programs certain common elements of experience on the emotional and social levels of life.

This kind of realist is not to be confused with the aristocrat; he is a stout defender of the principle of equality of educational opportunity. "A school structure which avoids division and differentiation," says Ulich, "involves the danger that there may be no quality in the equality (which would be the end of justice). . . . A school structure which emphasizes the idea of selection . . . carries with it the danger that the principle of equality might be disregarded (which would be the end of democracy). *The tension and friction* [between these two emphases] *is the essential challenge in the educational situation of democracy.*"

In other words, the democratic principle is to be satisfied by an equal quantity of basic schooling for all, while justice is to be satisfied by differentiation in the kinds of advanced schooling for children of differing abilities. Our obligation to democracy and equality, says Ulich, should not be based on a mistaken sense of equality contradictory to nature or society and should not lead us to deny man's inequality with respect to talent. Given this inequality, there is nothing unjust in the fact that "for the richly endowed the share will be greater than for the less privileged."

The idealist, condemning differentiation across the board, is at sharper odds with the first of the realist positions, which accepts differentiation because of existing social and economic inequalities, than he is with the second, which argues exclusively from natural capacity. In opposing the first position, the idealist points to its full flowering in Europe, where even in

supposedly democratic countries children are divided after six
to eight years of schooling on the basis not primarily of talent
but of social and economic standing. The rich and well-born
(or, at least, well placed) go on to secondary school and university, while the great mass of the children are sent to trade
school and apprenticeship. The division is not nearly so sharp
in America as in Europe. It is nonetheless, says the idealist, self-
evidently undemocratic.

Proceeding from this point, the idealist now trains his guns
on the second realist position (typified by Professor Ulich).
Democracy being a just social order, the idealist sees no distinction, in a true democracy, between the demands of democracy
and justice; where such a distinction can be made on the basis
of the existing situation, the existing situation is to that extent
undemocratic, and its reform lies in the sphere of political principle and political action, not in squaring the policies of education with an undemocratic political situation. The equality
of democracy, says the idealist, springs from the essential
equality of all men, in that all men possess the quality of humanity. Each possesses the same dignity as every other, the same
natural rights and responsibilities upon which democracy and
democratic citizenship rest. And this humanity, this dignity,
and therefore these rights and responsibilities, are not quantitative but qualitative. They make man man, and no man is
more human than another. Democracy is possible because every man has the powers of reason and of moral and political
choice. The function of education is to develop these powers
that are common to all men; the content of education must
therefore be common.

The idealist grants that there are natural inequalities, but he
maintains that they are quantitative, not qualitative, inequalities of degree and amount and not of kind. One man—or child—
has more or less of each of the human powers which all men
possess. It follows that differentiation in education must also be

quantitative and not qualitative, children of more or less ability acquiring different amounts of the same kind of education. The important word here is "acquiring." The idealist does not say that children of different amounts of ability should be given different lengths of schooling. The period of general education—which in his view should be compulsory through college or junior college—should be the same for all children. Since children are capable of acquiring different amounts of the same kind of education, the ideal should be a system in which each can acquire the maximum of which he is capable. It may take Sam all fourteen years—if that is the limit of compulsory education—to acquire what Joe got in twelve, or ten; Joe will then remain in school for all fourteen years, getting two or four additional years of the same kind of education.

The idealist knows that this is a big order; he does not know how it is to be filled; he admits it has never been tried; and he admits that, until the attempt has been made by every means that can be devised and tested, we shall never know whether the possibility can be realized. Short of this attempt, he knows that he cannot disprove the realist argument that the application of his principle might require one teacher per pupil and leave some students (capable of acquiring ever more liberal education) in school forever. If any such extreme turned out to be necessary, the idealist would, presumably, continue to maintain that, whatever the cost, we have got to prepare our children for democracy or abandon the democratic dream.

Of this the idealist is sure: that vocational education, as it ordinarily exists, is undemocratic and unjust. "Vocational education conceived as job-training," says Professor Sidney Hook, "represents the greatest threat to democratic education in our time. It is a threat to democracy because it tends to make the job-trained individual conscious only of his technological responsibilities, but not of his social responsibilities." Sir Richard Livingstone, former president of Corpus Christi College, Ox-

ford, defines a technician as "a man who understands everything about his job except its ultimate purpose and its place in
the order of the universe."

The idealist believes, in the words of John Dewey, that "any
scheme for vocational education which takes its point of departure from the industrial regime which now exists is likely
to assume and perpetuate its weaknesses, and thus to become an
instrument in accomplishing the feudal dogma of social pre-
determination." Moreover, to give the majority of children "an
education conceived mainly as specific trade preparation is to
treat the schools as an agency for transferring the older divisions of leisure and labor, culture and service, mind and body,
directing and directed class, into a society nominally democratic."

It is not just the training of workers for specific jobs in the
system of industrial production which the idealist condemns
but the inclusion in basic education of training for any specific
vocation, those that are highly technical and highly rewarded
as well as those that require minimum skills. Vocational—or
pre-professional—education during the period of basic schooling is undemocratic because it introduces differentiation at a
time when education should be the same for all. It is unjust because it interferes with the development to maximum capacity
of those powers which, in whatever degree, every human individual possesses in common with every other.

The responsibilities of citizenship are the same for all citizens
equally. There is, of course, a hierarchy of voluntary public
offices awarded, ideally, on the basis of superior talents; but
this system of award is thought to be just in so far as unequal
talents call for unequal responsibilities beyond those which all
citizens have in common. As for free time, its use, however
various and unequal the talents and interests of individuals, is,
in the idealist view, the same for all, in that it should involve
the leisure activities that result in mental and moral growth

throughout life: "The aim of education," says Dewey, "is to enable individuals to continue their education." But the idealist has to recognize what the realist recognizes fully: that, in addition to his future as a citizen and a man with time for leisure, every member of a just society is expected to do some work of the sort that earns his living. Here the idealist has to relate the whole of liberal education to the fact and function of human labor and, somehow, to the common and special vocations of men in an industrial democracy.

The "somehow" is the catch. The idealists are able to condemn vocational education for jobs as, in the words of John Dewey, "no better than animal training." They are able to condemn premature specialization—even in the learned professions —as interference with the maximum development of the individual's capacity to acquire liberal education. But when they try to relate that education to the vocations in which the future citizens will earn their living, their problem is harder. As an idealist, Bernard Iddings Bell proclaims our current education "lopsided" with vocationalism "to the point of absurdity." "The true aim of education," he maintains, "must consist in teaching *both* how to do a reputable job *and also* how to be a human being and enjoy life." But how to do it?

The idealist takes comfort here—much too easily, perhaps— in the testimony of occasional business, industrial, and professional leaders that the liberally educated man is more likely to rise than the vocational product. The vocationally educated graduate tends to be predetermined to a "job area" classification. He can be placed in an occupational category, and rise in that category, but he cannot readily move from one category to another; he is likely to remain a specialist, however highly placed and highly salaried, and to be excluded from the highest ranks of business, industrial, or professional life, from the ranks of the "generalists" who define and direct policy which, at the top levels, involves a comprehension of their own field as a whole and of all the related fields of human endeavor. He may become a vice-president of the company but he is not likely to become president; or a department manager, but not a general manager; or a chief engineer who is ordered by a "generalist" to tool up the plant for a new product.

"The most difficult problems American enterprise faces today," says Irving Olds, of United States Steel, "are neither scientific nor technical, but lie in the realm of what is embraced in a liberal arts education." The survival of our system, says Sidney Swensrud, chairman of Gulf Oil, depends on whether management can understand "the whole sweep of modern economic, political, and social life." Business, says *Fortune* magazine, can create its own specialists after it hires them, "but what it needs and can't create is men with a decent general education."

However moving this testimony, vocational and prematurely specialized education continues to flourish, with industrial organizations and the public exerting pressure for earlier and earlier and more and more intensive training for job "opportunities" achieved at the cost of ending one's education as an "uneducated specialist," in the expression of Robert Hutchins. A recent study shows that the proportion of college and university students majoring in the liberal arts and sciences dropped from 43 per cent of the graduating class in 1940 to 35.7 per cent in 1952. Among male students graduating in 1955 the proportion was 26 per cent, and even this was heavily weighted toward pre-professional studies having vocational purpose. The social sciences, having risen in brief popularity two decades ago, are now falling. The humanities have been falling for a long time and continue to fall.

More men in college today—one out of eight in all our colleges and universities, including graduate schools—are majoring in business than in anything else; the business course, the country over, has grown faster than any other; the clarion call of men like Olds and Swensrud is unheard. President Albert L. Nickerson of Socony Vacuum says that his company wants top employees whose education enables them to "understand the whole condition of man." But the utilization of school and college to narrow a man to a job proceeds unabated, "a tragedy," says Board Chairman William Benton of Encyclopaedia Britannica, "in its implications for American education, for American business, for American democracy, and for the young men themselves." The Commission on Human Resources and Advanced Training discovered that business undergraduates have a lower intelligence level than any other group of predominantly male students with the exception of physical education "majors." Vocational training attracts Canon Bell's "hewers of woods and drawers of water" and fixes them there.

At the lower occupational levels, vocational education has the appeal, to employers and administrators, of a continual flow of skilled and semiskilled technicians into the job market, in the professions no less than in business and industry, and, to employers and future employees, of the security of a calling in which "good steady jobs" are always likely to be available. The idealist contends against both these views; however desirable a flow of labor may be, however understandable the desire for economic security may be, the purpose of education is not first of all economic. It is first of all, he says, preparation for responsible citizenship, for an intelligent use of free time in the liberal activities of leisure, and for the humanization of necessary toil.

Vocational education and training have a long history of endowment by our federal government, while federal financial support of general education has been opposed as a threat to local school control. Long before the Civil War the decline of apprenticeship exerted pressure upon the schools to shoulder the burden of manual vocational preparation as they had once prepared the elite for the learned vocations. In 1862 the Morrill

Act provided for a grant of public land to each state to establish a college of agriculture and mechanic arts, and every state founded such an institution. The Smith-Hughes Vocational Education Act of 1917, giving aid to the states for agricultural, home economics, and industrial education, created a colossal vocational system at the secondary-school level, much expanded by both world wars and the depression of the early 1930's. National crisis, accounting for this whole development from 1862 on, has again been advanced during the Cold War as the reason for still further governmental encouragement.

Here again the question of the object of education arises. Is it to serve the individual and, through him, the society and the state, or is it to serve the advancement or security of the state directly? Chairman Lewis Strauss of the Atomic Energy Commission points out that between 1950 and 1960 the Soviet Union will have trained 1,200,000 new scientists and engineers and the United States 900,000. "If the crisis in education is not met," says Admiral Rickover, "we will be in danger of losing the Cold War by default." Are we to curtail liberal education because the Russians do? The realist says, "Yes." The idealist, recognizing that the question is, at bottom, political, argues that we lose the Cold War by default if we expand vocational education at the expense of liberal education. Liberal education and it alone, he says, is education for freedom.

Battered by the popularity of vocationalism, unable to prove (in the absence of vast experimentation) that the liberal education of every child is possible, the idealist is compelled to be the challenger. The realist is the champion, resting his case either passively on existing social and economic conditions (including those of the Cold War) or actively on his contention that liberal education for all is impossible because of natural inequalities. The facts of natural inequality, says the idealist, are not in fact known. The realist assumes them, and on this assumption accepts differentiation, just as the realist of a century ago assumed the "fact" of the ineducability of Negroes. And however great the actual range of natural capacities may prove to be, we do not know their educational significance, the idealist points out, because an undifferentiated liberal education for all children has never been tried.

But the idealist is left with another unanswered question: How is liberal education for all to be integrated with the life of labor which (along with citizenship and leisure) awaits every adolescent in a democracy? What means and what method —what kind of curriculum and what kind of content—are likeliest to relate undifferentiated schooling to the vocational future of the child? The question is not one of principle—on that the idealists are all agreed—but of policy. And here the idealists are at odds among themselves. And their differences on the level of policy, on the *means* of liberal education, embroil them in the question of the definition of liberal education itself.

CHAPTER 11

The Traditionalist and the Modernist

The democratic realist now yields the stage to the democratic idealists for their own controversy. The idealists, all of them accepting undifferentiated liberal education for all, are split by the question, What *is* liberal education? Is it in fact the same today, when it is to be given to all in a modern democracy, as it was yesterday, when it was given to a few in pre-democratic societies? Is its aim the same? Are its content and methods the same? The realist has a stake in this question in so far as he is concerned with liberal education during the years of schooling prior to differentiation; but for the idealists the issue is crucial.

The traditionalist—as his designation implies—maintains that the traditional policies of liberal education are as valid for the industrial, democratic present as they were for the non-industrial aristocracy of the past. What was once the best education for the few is now the best education for the many. In essential aim and in essential content, liberal education is unchanged. It consists in the cultivation of the intellect, the refinement of taste, and, indirectly, the development of character and personality through the mastery of the liberal arts and the study of the basic problems of man and society, past as well as present.

According to the traditionalist, the old distinction between the few and the many (as it affected educational opportunity) rested upon social and economic, not natural, inequality. So did the distinction as regarded the franchise. This distinction having been removed from the franchise, it should be removed from education. The aim of the liberal education of the few was the enrichment of the free life of citizenship, learning, and leisure, when only the few were destined for those blessings. Now that very child is so destined, the education that was appropriate for the few is appropriate for all. Only if the least gifted (or those who now appear to be least gifted) are offered as much of the same kind of schooling as the most gifted and leave school only when they have absorbed as much of it as they can—only thus is the democratic principle of equal educational opportunity satisfied.

Here we must revert, briefly, to a point made earlier. Throughout the whole variety and succession of pre-industrial societies, all of them undemocratic, the aim and content of liberal education remained substantially the same and substantially unchallenged. The greatest minds of their times and places were, at one time or another, focused on education. We may say that they were all of them wrong, century after century. But unless we take so extreme a position, we are compelled to concede that, under conditions which no longer exist, it was the best product of the best thinking of the ages preceding our own.

The primary aim, then, of basic schooling for all is, in the traditionalists' view, preparation for citizenship and leisure, including, of course, the continuation of learning. But the future citizen and man of leisure is also a future worker, and his schooling has to be related, at least indirectly, to his vocational future. Indirectly—yes, says the traditionalist; directly—never. Specific vocational education (and the differentiation it would introduce) has no place in the common school.

"If we say," writes Alexander Meiklejohn, former president of Amherst College, "that a given type of liberal education is 'non-vocational,' the statement needs sharp definition. It is one thing to say that liberal education must be deeply concerned with the vocations of men. It is an altogether different thing to say that the liberal learning of each pupil must be centered upon the specific vocation of that pupil." The first statement is true, says Meiklejohn; the second false and educationally disastrous. He continues:

If we assume that liberal teaching intends to equip a student to understand the human situation, who can doubt that a major part of his interest must go to the trades and professions of men? No one can understand the modern age or any other age unless he understands, both in idea and fact, the sciences and technologies by which the life of that age is sustained and determined. Such knowledge, may I add, is not, in a democracy, the privilege of an upper-class few. It is the necessary intellectual equipment of every citizen of a free society. Such study of the vocations of men is not vocational. It is liberal. A liberal college tries to understand and to teach how men make their livings. It does not teach any one man how to make his living.

The traditionalists do not believe that the content or method of liberal education has to be changed essentially from its traditional form in order to relate it to the vocational future of the child. They would have it serve the purpose—a purpose secondary to citizenship and the activities of leisure—of liberalizing or humanizing all forms of labor. But they think that this pur-

pose should be served indirectly, first, in so far as liberal education affords some understanding of the social, moral, political,
technical, and historical background and significance of labor
in an industrial democracy and, second, in so far as it provides
the kind of insight needed to solve the still-far-from-solved
problem of liberalizing and humanizing human labor.

What does it mean to talk about the "liberalization and humanization of labor" in the second half of the twentieth century? Does it mean anything at all? On this point traditionalists
as a whole (and many modernists with them) see the mechanization of labor as a problem of terrifying magnitude. As mechanization is more and more fully developed—short of absolute
automaticity—and the division of labor more and more finely
drawn, the satisfaction of the job itself diminishes or disap-
pears altogether. The man who instals the same screw a thousand times a day as a conveyor belt moves by him is engaged
in a form of labor which, however highly paid, defies liberalization or humanization. He is not an artisan; he is an adjunct
to a machine which, when his human error or his human imagination or his human individuality clogs it, turns on him and
says, "If I could only get rid of you, if only I had a mechanical
attachment to replace you, I wouldn't be in this jam." As Bernard Iddings Bell says:

Man exists to do creatively, in the most craftsmanlike manner
possible, all things that must be done: great things like government, or mothering, or the healing of minds and bodies; small
things like making beds, or hoeing corn, or driving a truck; things
in the public eye like making speeches, or unleashing atomic
energy, or making peace; obscure things like selling groceries, or
running a bus, or teaching school. He finds inner peace who works
at whatever is in front of him, not for the pay he gets or for what
he can buy with that pay, not for applause or gratitude, but for
sheer joy in creativity. There are a vast number of tasks to be
performed in this world, most of them not romantic. They may
be done in one of two ways: just to get them over with as quickly

and as painlessly as possible, in which case they become a monotonous burden hard to bear; or each as beautifully and thoroughly as possible, in which case life is good to the taste.

Our fathers knew the joy that lies in craftsmanship. They did not advocate it; they took it for granted. We have forgotten it, overlooked it. Craftsmanship is no longer practiced, taught, or praised. It is less and loss possible to get, for love or money, anyone willing to do an honest job of work. That is why we are restless, unreliable, combative, caught in a web of doubt and dismay. No salmagundi made of things, amusements, lust for power can assuage the gnawing hunger to create. There will be no recovery of serenity, no mutual patience sufficient for fraternity, until we learn ourselves and teach our boys and girls that unless human beings become creative artists they remain petulant children, dangerous, predatory.

Educators, employers, and workers themselves are aware of this colossal problem, and none of them sees an easy solution of it, or, indeed, any real solution at all. It is a fundamental problem, not of education, but of modern industrial democracy as a whole. The number of working hours per week in America has fallen from seventy at the beginning of the revolution of 1850–1950 to forty now—and the forty-hour-a-week worker produces six times as much as his ancestor working almost twice as long. And the trend proceeds; almost half the country's office workers put in fewer than forty hours. This shortened week is standard for most workers in brewing, baking, rubber, publishing, and the building trades, and the United Automobile Workers talks about new negotiations for a thirty-two-hour week. But the work, however far reduced, remains stultifying and, as automation advances, becomes ever more so.

If the problem is inherently insoluble, and if the only possible substitute for a solution is an ever decreasing amount of time on the job, the contribution of education obviously must be the continuing development of the principle upheld by both the traditionalist and the modernist: preparation for the ever more rewarding activities of leisure. If satisfaction is not going to be found on the job, it must be found off it. Doing what? Watching television, as the inhabitants of thirty-nine million of the nation's forty-six million homes now watch it—for an average (according to the estimate of the A. C. Nielsen Company) of five hours and twenty-six minutes a day? Gardening? Golfing? "It is hard to tell," says Robert Bendiner, in an article entitled "Could You Stand a Four-Hour Week?" "whether we are headed for an Elysium of culture that will put the ancient Greeks in the shade or for a hell of mass boredom modified by home-carpentry, hi-fi, plush motels, and ping-pong."

"Most men," says Professor Sumner Slichter of Harvard, "are not prepared to make good use of large and sudden additions to their leisure." President Emeritus William Russell of Teachers College, Columbia University, is even gloomier. "Too much leisure with too much money," he says, "has been the dread of societies across the ages. That is when nations cave in from within." And sociologists David Riesman and Warner Bloomberg, Jr., who also use the word "leisure" as a synonym for "free time," ask if we are now "not at least as unprepared for the 'life of Riley' " as we were for the coming of the factory.

In the face of these horrors—probable or possible—the traditionalist insists that liberal education must hold the line more firmly than ever against vocationalism. To address itself other than indirectly to the child's vocational future is to deprive that child in some degree of the humanizing elements of liberal education and to try, inadequately, to prepare him for a job which may itself be proof against humanization and for which schooling is not needed in any case. The best preparation for most of the jobs that most children will some day have in an industrial society is training on the job itself. "Unless," Robert Bendiner writes, "our whole educational system soon addresses itself to developing a nation of rounded amateurs, we shall only be creating more and more time for people who have less and less need of it. And the emphasis of that educational system is still overwhelmingly on professionalism and specialization rather than the humanities."

The traditionalist opposes any effort either to integrate liberal and vocational education or to educate through occupational activity as a part of schooling. He insists that any such effort necessarily dilutes the curriculum, thereby submitting the child to the soup-watering process condemned by Professor Bestor, and willy-nilly introduces the job-training which both the traditionalist and the modernist deplore. The quarrel between the two begins to take shape now, for the modernist holds that it is necessary, somehow, to integrate the two kinds of education in one common program and to familiarize the child with occupational activity through its introduction into liberal education. The traditionalist, in opposing this process, is not thinking of the alternating job-and-study schedule of schools like Antioch College, where, presumably, the purpose of the job is not specifically vocational; but he would oppose the Antioch kind of plan if it reduced the amount of time available to the liberal curriculum.

Preservation of the traditional liberal education, essentially unchanged, is unreasonable and unrealizable, says the modernist, in a world as radically changed from all worlds past as ours is. It not only should not be attempted; it cannot be, for it will not work. Granted the appropriateness of the traditional liberal program to its time and place, it is hopeless to suppose that it can be transmitted to the whole adolescent generation in present-day America, to thirty million children with their immense diversity of backgrounds, capacities, talents, and interests.

To the modernists' contention that it cannot be done—and apart from the desirability of trying to do it—the traditionalist can only reply that the teaching profession has never faced the problem of trying to do it and has, therefore, never used its resources to devise the technical means, the materials, and methods, for getting it done. Differentiation and vocational education, says the traditionalist, far from solving the problem, simply avoid it. The problem is to find out how to give every child a liberal education, and as much of it as he can take.

We have to discover equivalent materials—equivalent in the sense that they serve the same aim effectively—for giving a liberal education to children of unequal capacities or of different talents or tendencies. The "hand-minded"—granting for the sake of argument that there are such—may have to use different materials from the "book-minded"; if so, the materials must be found by experimentation. Equivalent methods, too, may have to be found. But the educative objective must be the same for every child and, in so far as content is inseparable from objective, the content, too. There is no limit to the differentiation of materials and methods as long as the kind of school and the kind of education are the same.

The traditionalist admits that the problem is immense. He admits that it has never been solved or even approached. He admits that he does not know how to solve it. But he insists that this is the problem—the discovery of materials and methods for giving every child an undiluted liberal education—and that the solution of this problem is the cornerstone of educational democracy. And not only of educational democracy; if, says the traditionalist, we cannot give a liberal education to every child, political democracy is a delusion, and the aristocrats are right.

The modernist accuses the traditionalist of repudiating the American revolution of the past century. How can the traditionalist say, on the one hand, that human society has been revolutionized by democracy, industry, and science and, on the other, that the education appropriate to pre-industrial aristocracy or feudalism is appropriate today? The modernist agrees that every child must have a liberal education, designed to prepare him for citizenship and the intelligent use of free time. But he cannot accept the traditionalist's exclusion from that education of a direct concern with the vocational aspects of life. "A truly liberal, and liberating, education," says John Dewey, here taking the modernist position, "would refuse today to isolate vocational training on any of its levels from a continuous education in the social, moral, and scientific contexts within which wisely administered callings and professions must function."

The fact that the traditionalists would have education directly concerned with citizenship and leisure and only indirectly with labor shows that they think of labor as separable from the other two activities and inferior to them. This separation and stigmatization, as the modernists see the traditionalist position, is worse than an inadequate approach to modern life. It is, they say, a regression to the outlook that characterized aristocracy and the slave society, where the few were destined for citizenship and leisure and the many for unrelieved drudgery. In effect, it denies the parity of the life of labor with the life of politics and thought and feeling and, in doing so, denies the principle of human equality.

Traditionalism, says the modernist, is a cover for the glorification and revivification of the past, for the maintenance or restoration of class distinctions. If the revolution of the past century means anything, it means that the character of liberal education has got to be altered to conform to modern conditions. It must concern itself directly with the child's vocational future. How? By integrating liberal and vocational education at every level. But again—how?

Here the modernist is in something of the tradionalist's dilemma. He does not know exactly how. Like the traditionalist, he rejects job-training out of hand, condemning current vocational practices in education as a perversion of the preparation of free men for free labor. But when it comes to specifying the means, methods, and materials of integrating liberal and vocational education, the modernist can only assert that it has never been tried, that it must be tried, that experimentation of every sort along these lines is the first order of education.

One recommendation of the modernist—which the traditionalist spurns—is the introduction of vocational interests into liberal education through the practice of different kinds of occupations within the basic curriculum. Another—and here the traditionalist is not in adamant opposition, although he may have reservations—is the liberalization of vocational education by the inclusion of social, historical, and ethical questions relevant to the vocation. "An education," says Dewey, "which acknowledges the full intellectual and social meaning of a vocation would include instruction in the historic background of present conditions; training in science to give intelligence and initiative in dealing with the materals and agencies of production; and study of economics, civics, and politics to bring the future worker into touch with the problems of the day and the various methods for its improvement. Above all, it would train power of readaptation to changing conditions so that future workers would not become blindly subject to a fate imposed on them."

The modernists, like the traditionalists, are, on the whole, insistent that the same kind or quality of education be given every child. The question which confronts them both is how this can be done when children are of such radically different backgrounds, capacities, talents, and interests. This is the question for which the traditionalist has no answer. He says that we must find out how but that somehow it must be done. Here the modernist thinks he has an answer. The integration of liberal and vocational education is that answer, at least in so far as some children may respond more readily to the use of machinery, for example, than to books. The integrated program would, by definition, have a broader basis of appeal.

But, says the modernist, the desirable integration between

liberal and vocational education cannot be achieved until schools and colleges revolutionize their entire attitude toward the vocational future of the student. The modernist admits that the difficulties of giving organizational form to this integrated curriculum are tremendous. But they must be faced for democracy's sake. Without a schooling that prepares the child for industrial democracy, in which labor and the problems of labor are as important as citizenship and the creative activities of leisure, democracy in an age of industry and science is impossible.

Thus both the traditionalist and the modernist argue their position on the basis of democratic idealism. One would suppose, since they stand together against both the aristocrat and the realist, that they stand fairly close together. Far from it; the quarrel between these two is the most violent in American education. "Traditionalist" and "modernist" are the mildest epithets with which they designate each other. The traditionalist accuses the modernist of assuming that the world began yesterday, and the modernist accuses the traditionalist of assuming that it ended a century or two ago.

That their quarrel should be violent is understandable in more ways than one. The very fact that they stand together in their democratic idealism gives the character of a civil war—a conflict between brothers—to the controversy. Together they represent the dynamic approach to the problem of American education; between them they come close to monopolizing current educational thinking (or, at least, talking), although the aristocrat and the realist are far from dead in theory and very much alive in educational practice. But it is the two kinds of democratic idealists who are the reformers, the crusaders for radical change from the present, largely realist, practices. It is no wonder that they clash more noisily with each other than does either of them with their common opponents.

But their quarrel is in itself basic, because it involves an issue that affects the character (and even more the content) of liberal education as much as the issue of vocationalism. The issue between them can be loosely expressed as that between science and philosophy. The culture in which liberal education developed and flourished was not only pre-industrial; it was, in large measure, pre-scientific. The culture in which we live is not only industrial; it is, in triumphant measure, scientific. What is the effect on liberal education of the difference between the culture of pre-scientific ages and that of an age of science?

No reasonable observer of the current educational scene would maintain that the traditionalist, as we have located him in the controversy, excludes scientific thought or modern science and technology from the program he proposes, any more than any reasonable observer would say that the modernist position excludes philosophy. The issue involving science and philosophy cannot be placed in the categories of dispute with which we have dealt up to this point. It engages them, to be sure, but not on the basis of simple confrontation of any of the three pairs of positions we have examined.

So it has to be dealt with independently, touching, as it does, all the current controversies in education. Its relevance to the organization of the school system (including the college), to adult education, and to the preparation of teachers can be indicated briefly in the following chapters dealing with the controversies on those three subjects. But in so far as it involves philosophical questions underlying every educational issue, and especially those regarding the organization, aims, and activities of the university, it will be examined in Part V of this book.

PART IV

The Issues in Action

CHAPTER 12

The School System

When we argue about education, the argument ordinarily centers on the education of our children, on what we call the school system, including, in the United States, the junior college and the college. And our view of the school system largely determines our thinking about adult education, research and professional training, and the preparation of teachers. In attempting to delineate the issues in education generally, the authors have had to deal with the school system considerably in the foregoing chapters. We have still to take note of certain questions about the organization of the system that arise from the controversy about differentiation and the relationship of liberal and vocational education.

These questions of organization deal essentially with practice rather than principle and must, therefore, be answered in administrative terms on the basis of ascertainable facts of time, place, and prevailing conditions. Important as they are, they are subordinate to the major issues and need not be discussed here in detail. They are three in number. The first is the question of the extent of basic schooling. The second is the question of the divisions of the educational system. And the third, arising from the first two, is the question of the place and character of the college.

As regards the first, there have been extensive changes in recent years without, however, any clear pattern beyond the tendency to push special education (vocational, technical, preprofessional) ever lower into the grades, to the disadvantage of basic schooling. It is fairly clear that this tendency, in all its variations, is largely the consequence of external pressures rather than of educational thinking. The extent of basic schooling—by which we mean general education common to all the students—has in many localities been affected by the job needs of new industries and by the consideration of the peacetime conscription of eighteen-year-olds into the army.

The shift away from the old 8–4–4 division of the school system has been steadier and more coherent, with the emergence of the two-year junior college and, more recently, the junior high school as a seventh- and eighth-grade unit. The junior college has been largely (and sometimes wholly) motivated as an accommodation of day students who will terminate their formal education there. The junior high school has had a more explicit purpose, as an experiment in bridging the curricular and emotional gaps between the elementary- and secondary-school environments.

The third question—that of place and character of the college—has had some attention in discussion but very little in practice. The experiments at St. John's College and the University of Chicago, with their prescribed curriculum of liberal education and their admission of students on the basis of readiness rather than the possession of a high-school diploma, have had some impact on a few colleges, but the college system as a whole has gone on undisturbed, except, of course, for increased enrolment and increasing emphasis on specialized and vocational teaching.

THE EXTENT OF BASIC SCHOOLING

Does the existing organization, with a compulsory phase for all and a voluntary phase for some, accord with the length of time for which undifferentiated education ought to be given to all? How long, in a word, should basic schooling last?

Here again the realist and the idealist are at odds. The realist acquiesces in the existing arrangement—or variety of arrangements—or approves of it with modifications. The present period of compulsory schooling, through two or four years of high school, tends now to extend beyond the period of undifferentiated education and, in the realist view, includes an adequate period of basic schooling for all. Higher liberal education (in effect, a continuation of basic schooling) should therefore continue to be voluntary and only for some, not all, of the high-school graduates. As a democrat, the realist would, of course, make higher education economically available to every qualified child.

The idealist thinks that differentiation can be postponed much longer than the realist assumes—indeed, until the very end of the present public school system, which culminates with the college degree. The period of basic schooling should be coextensive with whatever period is required for the education that now ends with the B.A. degree, whether that period is sixteen years or fewer. If, then, basic, undifferentiated schooling can be extended over a longer period than it now occupies, compulsory (or at least completely free) basic education should be given for the entire period.

How many years should undifferentiated schooling take?

The realist has already given his answer: up to eight, or perhaps ten or twelve. On this point there is diversity of opinion in the realist camp, but the existing practices, or some modification of them, are accepted, along with the present college termination date. The idealist, believing as he does that undifferentiated schooling can and therefore should be given for a very much longer period, believing, too, as a democrat, that the economic burden on both the individual and the community should not be so heavy as to exclude any child from any part of such schooling, proposes to shorten the period from first grade through the present four-year college by two years or even more. He maintains that much "wind and water"—in the form of duplication and superfluous subjects—can be squeezed out of the present system.

THE DIVISIONS OF THE SYSTEM

Should the present prevailing system of 8–4–4 years be retained or altered? On this question thinking is so diversified as to defy any characterization of position, but the following statement of related principles and their contraries may indicate the relationship of the larger issues to the question:

Suppose the principles to be (1) that differentiation cannot be postponed much beyond the present elementary school, if that long, and (2) that the human inequalities which necessitate differentiation also justify different amounts of schooling for different children beyond the point of differentiation or beyond the end of compulsory attendance. On these two principles it can be argued that the first division in the school system should be approximately at the point of differentiation; after that, relatively short divisions should allow children of different abilities to complete different sequences of short-term periods of advanced schooling. To meet these requirements, the present system, or minor modifications of it, would be adequate. All children complete basic schooling at, say, the seventh or eighth grade; some go on to finish junior high school, some of these to finish senior high school, and some of these terminate their formal education with two years of junior college, while some, after high school, enter a four-year institution.

Suppose the contrary to the two principles above: (1) differentiation in kind and aim of education can and should be eliminated altogether, right through college, and (2) human inequalities, remediable through the use of equivalent methods and materials, do not prevent any normal child from absorbing the same amount of basic schooling as any other. On this pair of related principles, even the present three units of elementary, secondary, and collegiate education are one too many. Since the entire school system provides a basic education, the only justifiable division is one between a preparatory or elementary phase and an advanced phase. The advanced phase would terminate basic education for all and would be preparatory only for that small proportion of students interested in higher education, in specialized training or research.

THE PLACE OF THE COLLEGE

The question of organization of the school system culminates in the college, taken as an integral part of the system and separated in function, if not in location, from the university as an institution for specialized training and research. It should suffice here to state the principal points of current debate on the place and character of the college, since the answers will be largely determined by the positions the disputants take on the issues of differentiation, the extent of basic schooling, and the divisions of the school system.

Should the public school system, both compulsory and noncompulsory, end at the average age of eigthteen, twenty, or twenty-two? Does the college belong to basic schooling or to higher education? Is its purpose distinct from that of secondary education, or is it distinct only as a phase of basic schooling?

Should the college be a four-year unit or a two-year unit, or should there be both? Should there be a division within the four-year college, with two years of general education (either the traditionalists' liberal program or the modernists' integrated liberal and vocational program) followed by two years of specialization, or should there be a four-year program? Should the college program consist entirely of a prescribed course of study or combine some required studies with electives (on the basis of either the "free elective" or "controlled elective" system)?

Our thinking here is necessarily circular; according to our different views of the role of college education, we shall be compelled to decide what the purpose of prior schooling should be. Should it be preparation for college, with college as the terminal phase of basic schooling? Or should it terminate basic schooling for all, preparing some for an advanced education?

Arguing that nothing will avail short of "a radical reorganization of our entire grade structure," Professor Paul Woodring of Western Washington College of Education, in his recent book, *A Fourth of a Nation*, makes a sharply detailed proposal for a "three-track" system, beginning with an ungraded primary school admitting children as young as five and keeping them for two or three years, with increasing stress on reading. Between seven and nine—whenever the individual is ready—the children will proceed to a four-year elementary school, and from there to high school at twelve or thirteen. Here they will be divided (but not "frozen") into three groups, average, above average, and below average, and the same student may, according to his ability in each subject, be in different groups.

At sixteen or seventeen, upon high-school graduation, those who have no further aptitude for academic work will leave school for a job; a second group, of intermediate learning capacity, will attend a trade school or all-purpose junior college for a year or two, then go to work. The third group will enter a four-year liberal arts college offering no vocational or pre-professional training whatever; and most of the college graduates will go on to two years or more of university or professional school, at age twenty. All future teachers will, *after* the four-year college, take the M.A. degree in two years of teaching preparation.

Woodring demonstrates that none of these separate changes from the present system is new, either in theory or in practice, and he holds that where they have failed in practice it is because they have had to be introduced piecemeal into individual schools and incongruously with the prevailing system. What is needed is reorganization of the system *as a whole;* there is no other way to break the circle. But the circularity in educational thought persists—as Woodring recognizes—in respect to content. And here we see that general education (liberal or integrated liberal and vocational) cannot be argued apart from the consideration, in Part V of this book, of the transition from the pre-scientific past to the age of science.

CHAPTER 13

Learning Begins at Forty

In his study of the "new leisure" in America, Robert Bendiner, under the title "Could You Stand a Four-Day Week?" writes as follows:

In the main it will take all the educational facilities of the country to create the new climate, and here again, I think, there is need to break loose from old concepts. With time available throughout a man's existence, why should education, even in its formal sense, be confined to the first twenty years or so? It might be well to let some restless youngsters get into the working force at fifteen if they wish, rather than have them turn to juvenile delinquency out of boredom, and then bring them back to school at twenty-five, when they are mature enough to want to learn. Others might proceed pretty much along present lines, and still others could return to school intermittently over the years, either for the purpose of changing their occupations or simply to expand their horizons.

Sooner or later we shall have to shake off the whole tradition of "terminal education," I was told by Dr. Clarence Faust, who heads the Fund for the Advancement of Education. "We have to get rid of concepts like graduation and all the phraseology that suggests that education has fixed limits. 'Where did you get your education?' we ask a man, and the answer will be, 'At Yale'—as though it come done up in a package."

The need is for more than adult classes or extension courses such as we now have. It is for a fresh concept altogether—a national interest in continuous education, through a combination of formal institutions, specialized televison, discussion groups like the Great Books, and, perhaps above all, the ancient method of person-to-person instruction. If leisure makes it possible for more and more people to learn, it can also provide more and more people to teach—people whose primary job may be in a bank or a shop but who, having acquired proficiency in a language or an art, find it pleasant and profitable to teach it to others.

Work, said Aristotle, is for the sake of leisure; and in answer to the question, "What ought we to do when at leisure?" he immediately went on to say that "we ought not to be amusing ourselves." He thought of amusements or recreations as medicine for removing the fatigues or strains caused by hard work and thus preparing for more hard work. Play, in short, is for the sake of work, as toil is for the sake of leisure. But what should occupy the free time of those who are fortunate enough not to have to toil in order to gain their subsistence? Aristotle's answer was that "those who are in a position which places them above toil [should] occupy themselves with philosophy or with politics," which, more freely translated, means that they should engage in the creative work of the liberal arts and sciences, of citizenship and statecraft.

Leisure is thus a higher or nobler kind of work than toil, just as the goods it produces (those of civilization and of the human spirit) are higher or nobler than the goods produced by toil (those of subsistence or of the body). But, like toil, leisure is work, not idleness or play. Above all, it is not to be confused with "free time," which is nothing but the time left unused by sleep or toil—time which can be squandered in idleness or usefully employed *either* in play and recreation *or* in leisure-work. In Aristotle's view, it would be possible to say that a man who was not liberally educated for the use of his free time in leisure-work might have too much free time on his hands for his own good; but it would not be possible to say that a man had too much leisure, any more than it is possible to say that he could have too much virtue.

In America today most people use the words "leisure" and "free time" as if they were synonymous, and they do not distinguish between leisure-work and play or recreation as quite opposite ways of using free time. The current view is that a free man's free time is his own to use as he pleases. He cannot be told what he *should* do with it for his own good or the good of his society. A people with "leisure time" (i.e., free time) may have as many different ways of spending it as there are persons. One fishes; another plays cards or chess; another "putters around the house"; another has any one (or more) of a thousand hobbies; and another goes to the movies, the prize fights, or the night clubs or takes a walk or a ride. In a culture distinguished by the thickness and proliferation of its periodicals, many spend a good part of their free time in reading for current information or light entertainment. And some play horseshoes, and some breed fuchsias.

Some American adults spend their free time studying and learning an immense variety of useful or fine arts. Some read serious books seriously, but surprisingly few. In England, where education is still far from universal, 55 per cent of the adults can be found reading a book at any time; in the United States, the land of universal education, only 17 per cent are reading a book, *any* book. Of the books written, published, and purchased between 1945 and 1955, the top ten each sold more than three million copies apiece. What were they? Numbers one, two, three, four, five, six, and seven were titles by Mickey Spillane. Eighth was Fulton Oursler's *The Greatest Story Ever Told*, ninth *Betty Crocker's Picture Cook Book*, and tenth James Jones's *From Here to Eternity*. "One might brutally surmise," says former President Gordon Dupee of the Great Books Foundation, "that our culture is a culture of blood, guts, gastronomy, and a little God."

We should be surprised that Americans read fewer—and "faster-moving"—books than any other highly advanced people; surprised but not shocked. Ours is a society incredibly rich in amusements or diversions within the economic reach of all, a society, in addition, puritanically influenced in the direction of hard work. We are—again, par excellence—the people of the quick lunch, the long commutation trip, the day unbroken by the siesta, and the two-week building construction job. "Work is for the sake of leisure," but many Americans, thousands of whom are not economically needy, spend their free time working. To purchase the burgeoning apparatus needed to occupy themselves off the job, a rapidly increasing number of Americans are spending the time won by reduced working hours on a second, part-time job.

We should be surprised but not shocked to hear of our illiteracy in terms of adult self-education, and we should not be disheartened. If it is important—if the glory that was Greece and the grandeur that was Rome were not produced exclusively by light comedy or "do-it-yourself" kits—we should do something about it. And no other people are as well equipped to do something about it if they want to. Educators, with pardonable prejudice, think that education is important, including adult education. But their view is supported by the concept of a democratic society. A democracy is the only society that can be destroyed merely by the ignorance of its people, for its people are its sovereigns. The subject can live—politically—without education. The citizen cannot.

Why should free time be used for leisure rather than for play? The adult has the political necessity to learn and to go on learning. He also has the moral necessity, because he has to make moral choices all his life. Perhaps—this is arguable—there is not much new from age to age in the knowledge that underlies moral choice. But what is old takes a lifetime of study to learn, and if there is anything new discovered (and such fields as criminology and child psychology suggest that there is, continually), every adult ought to know it for his own, his children's, and his community's good.

Man has a psychological necessity to go on learning, a necessity perhaps more basic even than his moral and political need. Without exercise the body becomes flabby and susceptible to disease, and, while different forms of exercise are appropriate to the different stages of physiological life, it is self-evident that some sort of bodily exercise is indispensable, even in old age. The mind, too, becomes flabby without exercise, and susceptible to "disease," that is, to partisanship, prejudice, and dogmatism in non-dogmatic matters. The unexercised mind, like the unexercised body, is unable to keep up with those around it. Left behind, it is reduced to solitude or to the deadly company of similarly unexercised minds, dependent on strong external stimulation and increasingly difficult to stimulate except by increasing the strength and dosage of the stimulant.

There is no exercise, as we know from our bodily experience, without effort. Reading the funnies is effortless. And staring at even the best television production—if no effort goes into doing it—is no more mental exercise than reading the funnies. The effort to master problems—mental hurdles—alone exercises the mind and keeps it growing. And while some mental functions are, like physical functions, affected by age, the most important appear to be much more resistant to the years than the body is. It is much rarer for a man who has been running all his life to be a runner at eighty than it is for a man who has been a thinker all his life to be a thinker at eighty. The physiological "peak" is reached in the twenties; the intellectual, decades later, if ever. It would be a supererogation to name the men who have produced their intellectual masterpieces in their sixties, seventies, and even (if their bodies sustained them) in their eighties.

Bertrand Russell, who at eighty-five is still making contributions to human knowledge in philosophy and political thought, said forty years ago:

> The same love of adventure which takes men to the South Pole, the same passion for a conclusive trial of strength which leads some men to welcome war, can find in creative thought an outlet which is neither wasteful nor cruel, but increases the dignity of man by incarnating in life some of that shining splendor which the human spirit is bringing down out of the unknown. To give this joy in a greater or less measure, to all who are capable of it, is the supreme end for which the education of the mind is to be valued. It will be said that the joy of mental adventure must be rare, that there are few who can appreciate it, and that ordinary education can take no account of so aristocratic a good. I do not believe this.

Why, he asks, is this "joy of mental adventure" so common in children, so rare in later life? "Because everything is done to kill it during education."

Adult learning would seem to be indicated by the moral, political, and psychological nature of the human case. Like the subordinate questions concerning the organization of the school system, many disputes in the sphere of adult education occur on the level of practice rather than of theory—disputes having to do with administration or with the use of various means and methods. But the basic controversy, which we shall deal with here, has to do with its aim and, consequently, with the kind of education that adult education should be. It involves only one fundamental opposition, and, although that opposition (like all issues in adult education) is less clearly defined in the literature of the subject than the controversies about the school system, it has the advantage of being singular.

The antecedent conditions of the controversy are, first, all six of those conditions of modern American life listed on page 71 of this book. But the adult education issue involves another, special condition of our modern life: the increasing availability—now to the point of universality—of adequate schooling in childhood and adolescence. The six common conditions of American life, plus the radical decline in immigration (and the increase in popular education in the emigrant countries), have all but eliminated the need, so acute only fifty years ago, to provide basic schooling for adults who were unschooled or very inadequately schooled in their youth. To the limited extent that such compensatory schooling is still with us, its purpose, character, and content involve the same issues as the school system, already discussed. Only its method—inasmuch as the pupils are adults—differentiates it from the school-system controversy.

So the distinction must be made sharply between what Sir Richard Livingstone calls "adult education for the uneducated and adult education for the educated." Our concern, in the present and prognosticated development of American society, is with adult education for the educated, that is, post-school learning to continue education beyond its termination in youth, or even beyond all institutional education, including the college and the university as well as the elementary and secondary schools.

The opposition in adult education so conceived begins with the aristocrat and the democrat. The contemporary (like the ancient) aristocrat holds that only a small proportion of mankind are genuinely educable, in either youth or maturity. These should receive education of such a character that they are equipped to continue learning throughout their lives. Given the truly aristocratic view—the separation of the virtuous and intelligent, not the rich or hereditarily noble, from the ineducable masses—those who are capable of being liberally educated will be of such disposition as to continue their own development in later life and can be relied upon to sustain and increase their own learning.

The democrat rejects the aristocrat's first principle. The equality of men requires equality of educational opportunity. But the democrat has, here again, to confront the facts or suppositions of inequality of backgrounds, capacities, talents, and interests among persons. And once more the democrats divide into realists and idealists. The realist believes that the largest part of the adult population cannot (or will not) engage in the kind of liberal learning which is a continuation of the liberal curriculum offered to the few in school and college. For the many, who, at the point of differentiation (which the realist accepts or approves), go on to vocational education, the appropriate adult education should be partly on the vocational and partly on the emotional and social side of the adult's life. For the few, who go on with liberal education through college, the appropriate adult program should, of course, be liberal in character. But here the realist tends to agree with the aristocrat that such persons can, on the whole, be left to take care of their adult education by themselves.

The democratic idealist disagrees radically with his realist brother and applies the precept of equal educational opportunity to adult education in the same way he applies it to the school system. In short, he thinks that it should be of the same kind for all. As in the case of the school system, it should not involve specific training for jobs but should be liberal in character, either in the traditionalist's or the modernist's version of liberal education. The democratic idealists are, of course, going to quarrel among themselves again, on the basis of the traditionalist and the modernist views, but before they do they want to present a united front long enough to make, with particular emphasis on adult education, a point they both made earlier.

All education, in the idealist view, is preparation for more education, for the lifetime of learning. Liberalism—in the sense in which it is applied to education—does not sustain itself after the adolescent human has received his degree of Bachelor of Liberal Arts. By definition, liberalism is (among other things) open-mindedness, and if, through life, the mind is open and nothing is going into it, it will wind up empty, or sterile, or— a little less metaphorically and a little more likely—it will wind up closed. Basic schooling is liberal only if it prepares the young for adult education, and adult education is liberal only if it prepares the mature for more education.

The life of the mind is learning, and it never ends. No man's education is complete, nor will it ever be; and if, contrary to possibility, it were, he would soon die intellectually. The satisfaction of school requirements—at any level—merely certifies that the individual is equipped to carry on learning in any sphere of knowledge or skill. There are things of the vastest importance for life that the young cannot learn; there are, as has often been pointed out, no infant prodigies in morals or politics. Life itself provides the materials and the struggle with those materials for learning and enjoying some of the things that, to the young, are "academic." The Bachelor of Arts is not yet wedded to them, and the Doctor of Philosophy is qualified only to practice a branch of continuing learning.

But what of the realist argument that most men cannot or will not go on learning, and his tendency to agree with the aristocrat that those who can do so can be trusted to do so by themselves? Here the idealist is inclined to yield to a thoroughly realistic view of modern industrial democracy, crowded with adult diversions and absorbed by the puritanical determination to "get ahead." Even the idealist will not quarrel too violently with the ancient aristocrat who, under aristo-

cratic pre-industrial conditions, held that those who had access
to a liberal education could be relied upon to continue it by
themselves. Under present conditions it is apparent to the
idealist that, of those who can go on with liberal education by
themselves and unaided, few will. Organized agencies have got
to provide such programs and, more than provide them, promote them, "sell them" assiduously, for adult education is voluntary and is competing in the market place with widely
advertised claims on the free time of the American adult.

Something more: even those adults who will go on with
their own education by themselves need organization, infor-
mal or formal. The mature person is, of course, much more
competent to study alone than the young, but a lifetime of
solitary study is lonely, ultimately discouraging in most cases,
and generally less rewarding than the kind of study that provides for the interaction of many minds on the same problem.
Man is sociable; he is also social. His social problems (and
even his personal problems have social implications) are more
intelligently (or at least more broadly) approached in company than in solitude. True, a book is company, or a picture
or a concerto, but they cannot talk back. They provide one
exchange of intercourse with the living individual; beyond
that, except as one mines them for deeper meaning, they cannot go on talking. Adult education, like basic schooling, has
got to be partly social; if men do not learn *from* one another,
at least they learn *with* one another.

On all these points the democratic idealists, whether they
take the traditionalist or the modernist position, see eye to eye.
They agree, too, that the problem of how to give an undifferentiated liberal education to adults may be even more difficult
than the problem of how to give such an education to every
child in school. Here, again, they insist that we do not know
that it cannot be done; we have never tried to do it. As in the
case of basic schooling, experimentation with equivalent mate-

rials and methods is urgent. The urgency is clear, if we believe that our form of government and society depends, for its preservation and improvement, on a populace which has not only gone to school but continues to engage in learning all its life; in that case, we have got to find out how to educate every adult.

But what kind of education? Here the idealists divide, as they do on the school system, between the traditionalist and the modernist positions. The modernist, at this as at the adolescent level, would integrate liberal education, not with vocationalism in the narrow sense of job-training, but directly with the current concerns of modern life, and especially vocational concerns. Adult education would still be liberal in aim, but its content would be much different from the program recommended by the traditionalist, namely, the historic program of liberal education modified to reflect the change from a prescientific, non-industrial, and non-democratic age to that of industrial democracy keyed to scientific development.

The difference between the two idealist positions—in adult as in adolescent education—is very bitterly argued, although it may appear to be much less radical than the difference between the idealists and the realists or the democrats and the aristocrats. It is essentially a difference in emphasis. The modernist would emphasize change and the conditions of contemporary society and its improvement, while the traditionalist would emphasize the enduring character of human nature and human society and place contemporary problems in the setting of the human tradition.

Which of these emphases is more appropriate for adults? Is the education of already educated adults different, in this respect, from that of children? We have already observed that adults are better able than children to understand, in the light of their experience of life, the great moral, political, and theological problems raised throughout the tradition of Western thought. They are in the midst of life. They read, they study, they talk in an atmosphere beset by current reality. Which do they need the more—and do they need it more or less than children: emphasis on the contemporary or emphasis on the enduring? Which emphasis will have more meaning for them, more lifelong usefulness and enjoyment? Which will hold their attention better? For we must remember that their education, unlike children's, is voluntary. The answers to these questions lie partly, to be sure, in the quality of the leadership they get and in the selection of materials and methods; but they lie partly in the realm of judgment as to human nature and its needs and satisfactions at the different stages of life. And here the traditionalists and the modernists differ.

But, on the whole, the basic opposition with regard to adult education is not to be stated in terms of the six positions we have tried to identify in connection with the other controversies in education. The reason is that adult education is so insignificant an institution in the United States, so vaguely and variously defined, and so eccentrically practiced, that the opposition is an implicit one rather than a matter of positions clearly held and debated. This opposition is, therefore, perhaps best stated in terms of a theory of adult education—of what it is held that it should be—in contrast to the whole body of prevailing practices in the field. This opposition discloses something like a minority view with a close affinity for the idealist's program of reform of the school system and a majority view (as reflected in the whole complex of present practices) with a close affinity for the realist's acquiescence in the existing arrangements.

General agreement among those who would reform adult education (or construct a genuine program, in contrast with the prevailing chaos) is found on the following "shoulds":

1. Adult education should be conceived as necessary for all persons after they have completed their adolescent schooling, because of the limitations on learning in youth and the conse-

quent deficiencies intrinsic to even the best schooling. It should, therefore, not be conceived as a form of schooling but rather as that part of the educational process which tries to complete what is barely begun in school.

2. Adult education undifferentiated in aim and quality should be conceived as possible for all persons, regardless of their inequalities, because the precept of equal educational opportunity implies the opportunity for all persons to receive the same kind of education, though their capacities to acquire it may differ in degree.

3. Adult education should be conceived as liberal in aim and content rather than vocational in the sense of job-training, and intellectual rather than moral or emotional, concerned with ideas and the pursuit of understanding and wisdom, because of the nature of human freedom and of human society.

4. Adult education should be conceived as interminable, a lifelong undertaking, because learning can never be completed and because the mind, if it does not live the life of learning, loses its vitality much as the unexercised body disintegrates.

5. Adult education should somehow be related to earning a living, citizenship, and the liberal activities of leisure-work, because the adult learner's role in the economy is of great importance both to him and to society, because he is a citizen with serious civic responsibilities, and because he is a man with ever increasing time for leisure-work.

The foregoing considerations lead irresistibly to the conclusion that post-institutional agencies and means of adult education must be devised, under public, private, or mixed auspices, to provide inducement and guidance for that large body of the adult population who, for whatever reason, will not carry on learning entirely under their own direction. Persuasion must play a large and continuous role because participation is not compulsory. The program, in so far as materials and methods are concerned, must be a continuing program, calculated to engage and interest its participants over a lifetime; if it is not, it can be justified only in so far as it arouses mature persons to begin some form of liberal adult education. And the numerous distinctions between such a program and the education of children should include the function of group leaders or directors, rather than teachers in the school-system sense, since the "teachers" and "pupils" are all equal as adults voluntarily engaged and not categorically distinguished in status.

When we turn from any such theory of adult education to the prevalent practices, we see at once how fundamentally different they are from such a theory—and from each other. We modern Americans are devoted to trial and error. We hesitate to adopt concepts of any kind as a guide to practice lest we find our freedom to experiment strait-jacketed. But we have had perhaps a century of experimentation with adult education, without a clear conception of what it is or what it should be, and we find ourselves with an ever increasing multiplication of offerings many of which, on any serious view of education (even vocational education), cannot be called educational at all. Impossible as it is to locate a theory underlying this immense tangle of practices, it is readily possible to discern a set of views, rarely articulated, that is common to almost all of them and contrary to the theory outlined above.

By and large, the existing forms of adult education suggest that the majority view among educators, especially those responsible for content at both the adult and the adolescent levels, tends to regard the completion of adolescent schooling as the completion of education. This view is manifested by all the efforts to construct a course of study which embraces, or tries to embrace, everything that ought to be known by an educated man or woman. The majority view among the students themselves, as well as their parents, tends to look upon the completion of school requirements as certification that education has been completed, and this is especially true, of course, as applied to the college curriculum. And the majority view, among educators, parents, and students, tends to regard liberal education (no less than vocational) as preparation either for specialized study or for vocational success, or even for the duties of citizenship, but not for a liberal use of free time in adult life—not, that is, for the continuation of learning.

The prevalent practices indicate, on the whole, disagreement with or disinterest in the proposition that the same kind of education is both necessary and possible for all adults and that it should be liberal and intellectual. Many, perhaps most, of the adult programs are neither liberal nor intellectual, and, along with most of those that are, they are offered on the basis of differing capacities and interests in the adult population. The proposition that education is an unending process is contradicted, in practice, by the prevalence of short-term programs unrelated to other programs in the adult field. And the common use of the teacher as such, together with methods and materials appropriate to the education of uneducated adults but not to that of the educated, suggests a general disinterest in the proposition that the "teacher" and the "pupil" are, in adult education, peers as adults whose prior education differs only in degree.

There is no intent here to say that the existing practices are right or wrong, but, rather, to discover among them some common basis that indicates a theory of adult education. In so far as we have been able to do this, we find that, on the whole, the practices and the theory they presuppose are contrary to the theory advanced by most of the educational reformers in the adult field and to both the traditionalist and the modernist views among democratic idealists. If the existing practices and theory are sound, the only problem is the improvement and extension of the present practices. If, however, they are unsound, the consequences of so holding are considerable with respect both to the school system and to adult education itself.

If the theory of reform is sound, the school system is affected in three ways. First, the aims of basic schooling must include the wise and profitable use of free time for leisure activities in adult life, such use to include continuing learning. Second, the content of basic schooling, especially at the secondary and collegiate levels, must be limited, on the view that not everything that has got to be learned in this life has got to be learned in school; nor should the expectation or insistence prevail that what is appropriately taught in school can be fully mastered in adolescence without re-examination in adult life. And, third, taking the first two together, the educational institution, including the college and even the university, cannot be regarded as terminal for liberal education but always and for everybody preparatory to the interminable life of liberal study.

A suggestive observation can be made here regarding the inclusion in basic schooling of the aim of the wise and liberal use of free time in adult life. There has been some revulsion against high-school and college football on a number of obvious grounds. One of the complaints is relevant here: that these are sports which cannot be played except in youth. It has been urged that greater emphasis be placed on the non-contact and "minor" sports that we can continue to play in middle and later life and even on sedentary games like chess. If the argument is valid with respect to athletics, the possibility at least exists that it is valid in the choice and emphasis of curricular subjects.

An indirect—but no less important—consequence for the school system of the reform of adult education would be its effect upon one aspect of the apparently unequal learning capacities of children: the inequality induced or perpetuated by the home environment rather than by nature. Children can be gravely handicapped by their parents' lack of education or, worse, lack of interest in the children's education. The parents' continuing education is even urged as a necessity in view of the present and projected shortage of school facilities. Professor Dwight L. Bolinger, chairman of the Romance Languages Department of the University of Southern California, observes that we Americans want our son or daughter to have "the best education that money can buy." He says, "Make sure of it by giving him what no money can buy—an attitude toward learning that will carry him past all the barriers that overcrowded colleges may set up. Do it by example, by displaying that attitude yourself, by leading him—and most of all, by accompanying him in his great intellectual adventure. . . . Give your child the interests that will help him in school by cultivating them in yourselves."

The "peer group" may be more influential with children, especially in their teens, than the older generation is, but children who come to their teens in a *learning* home are more likely to accept learning than those whose parents spend all their free time in light distractions. The parents' disinterest in learning (if, as in most American homes, it is not forced on them by economic stress) may arise from their own deficient schooling, but in our situation it is far more likely to arise from their culture's failure to interest them in learning, both because it bids high for their interest in non-educational diversions and because it fails to provide adequate adult education facilities.

The critical effect of the home on the supposed ability of the child to learn is indicated by the two-year study of a public school system by the Citizens' School Study Council of Fairfield, Connecticut. Author John Hersey, reporting the Council's conclusions, declares that one of the greatest of all current educational problems is the absence of what he calls "the urge to read." "Neither parents nor teachers," he writes, "do enough about fostering their children's inner urge to learn to read. . . . This is the area in which parents do the most harm and could do the most good. We believe that parents should create in the home an atmosphere that is conducive to reading. They should have good books and magazines at hand. Parents should read to children. They should try to entertain them with reading and make reading a pleasure, as television is a pleasure. If school is where learning to read belongs, home is where happiness in reading belongs." The idealist in the education controversy is particularly insistent that the reform of adult education may remove one considerable source of supposed inequality among children and affect the whole question of differentiation based upon inequality.

If the theory of the reform of adult education is sound, the practical organizational implications are tremendous. We should have to decide how to establish, arrange, and administer the post-institutional agencies and devise the technical means for carrying out the program in a way that is suitable for the whole range of adult circumstances. The problem would call for great ingenuity in the invention of new techniques and in the adaptation of present programs. This much is clear: if we conclude that liberal education for all is necessary, we can afford to spare no effort to make it possible and effective. But if the present practices are adequate to both the human and the national need, the problem of extending and improving them is largely financial, and the areas of educational controversy are reduced by one.

CHAPTER 14

The Learning of Teachers

Educational controversy involves two institutions which, chronologically, lie between the adolescent and the adult programs. One is what used to be called the normal school, the institution (or department of another institution) devoted to the preparation of teachers. The other is the university. In so far as the major issues regarding the university center on the transition from a pre-scientific to a scientific era, they will be reserved for Part V of this book; but the structure and function of the university are not wholly irrelevant to the problem of teacher-training.

No fact of education is more widely known than the fact that the richest country in the world has had an acute shortage of teachers for many years. And it is a country whose people believe that they believe fervently in education. For the past few years this shortage has been desperate, and, as the school population continues to rise, there is every evidence that the need will not decline for a long time. California, with 100,000 full-time teachers, began the 1957–58 school year with a shortage of 28,000, and its State Department of Education warned that the teacher-recruitment problem would be "critical" for the next decade. Professor Bolinger, examining the national shortage, says, "Even if we could recruit them, we could never train them in time." And Peter F. Drucker estimates that college and university faculties are losing 4,000 more teachers annually than they are acquiring—at a time when they will need an increase of 250,000 in the next twenty years.

Why are there too few teachers?

The answers, each of them partial, are many. In a country where, in contrast with the rest of the world, much teaching at the secondary level and almost all teaching at the elementary level is done by women, the extension of job opportunities for women in business and industry has placed teaching in a highly competitive category and at a sharp disadvantage. With infinitely less preparation and dedication a woman can get an easier and often better-paid job than schoolteaching. The teacher's hours, according to the National Education Association, are forty-eight a week, at a job than which there is none more taxing. The average wage is under $4,000 a year—a figure more meaningful, if less resounding, than that of the annual national expenditure on education—twelve billion dollars (which is less resounding when it is compared with thirteen billion on recreation and fourteen and a half on tobacco and alcohol).

Some hard facts appeared in the wake of the Russian *Sputniks*. We learned from Dr. William G. Carr, executive secretary of the National Education Association, that the U.S.S.R. spends 6 per cent of its national income on education, compared to our outlay of about 4.5; that Soviet schools have one teacher for every seventeen students, while ours "struggle to maintain a ratio of one to thirty"; and that teaching is one of the highest-paid professions in Russia and one of the lowest-paid in America.

It takes seven or eight years from college entrance to get a doctorate for college teaching—at a salary lower than the four-year graduate gets in business or industry. In addition (and again by way of contrast with the rest of the world), the profession of the teacher in America has been poorly rewarded in social status, doubtless because financial success and social acceptance, here as in any relatively new culture, have so readily been won without education. On balance, teaching does not appear to be worth its trouble to many of those best equipped to do it; three out of every four men and women who took the Ph.D. degree in chemistry in 1956–57 went into industry, and three out of every five who took the degree in physics.

But the most obvious reason for the teacher shortage has been the meteorically rising school population of the last fifty years, and especially of the last decade, with its "war babies." More pupils are staying in school, and those who used to stay are staying longer. California, with the biggest enrolment of all, ought to be constructing four elementary schools a week and four high schools a month to accommodate its almost three million public school pupils. And in twenty years the nation's college enrolment will be as big as its high-school enrolment of today.

Along with the insatiable demand for more teachers—a demand which itself has affected the character and quality of teacher-training—there are two other current conditions antecedent to the teacher-training issue. The first is the development, as the result of empirical research, of specialized knowledge in the field of education in the past half-century—in educational psychology and sociology, in testing, measuring, and other methods of evaluation, in school administration, etc. The second is the radical decline, over the same period, of undifferentiated general education in the schools and the colleges, in which the basic (as well as much of the advanced) training of teachers takes place; and the rise, until they now predominate, of specialized courses, vocational or other. "At the beginning of the century," says Professor Frederick Eby in his *Development of Modern Education*, "teacher training was chiefly historical and theoretical. Soon, however, schools added courses in methods and curriculum and, most significantly of all, 'practice teaching.' Today the training in methods and practice and in administration, measurements, and other practical lines has outrun the study of theory and subject matter."

So far as elementary and secondary schools are concerned (and especially the former), the great majority of teachers now in practice have received considerably less general education than is signified by the B.A. degree from a regular four-year college. Many of them entered a teachers' college directly from high school, or at the latest from junior college, and, even then, a considerable part of their last years of common schooling may have been devoted to specialized studies in the field of education itself rather than to general education.

True, we are now witnessing a limited revival of general education, side by side with the much less limited expansion of specialized training. It has appeared in a few secondary schools and in more than a few of our leading colleges and universities. And the amount of general education in teachers' colleges is definitely higher than it was a decade or two ago. But even the future teachers who are now being trained are receiving an education that is distinctly below the level and duration of general education offered in the colleges and universities where this trend has developed. Furthermore, the faculty qualifications in the general run of teacher-training institutions fall below the standard for instructors in the liberal arts colleges, and their professional as well as their economic status is correspondingly inferior.

This condition is thought to be justified in part by the development of educational science and research, the results of which, it is supposed, must be communicated to teachers in training, and in part by the need to prepare as many teachers as possible as rapidly as possible to start earning their living as soon as possible. The effect of this last pressure on the quality of teaching candidates may be indicated by the fact that, while 66 per cent of the entering students at Ohio State University were deficient in mathematics, the percentage so deficient in the College of Education was 82. These two facts—the necessity to teach special educational techniques and the necessity to speed up the production of teachers—are thought to militate against the requirement of four years of general education at the college level for all future teachers. And since many of them will teach vocational or specialized subjects, the tendency to reduce general education—in their cases at least—is still greater.

As far as college teaching is concerned, most instructors now in practice (except for the oldest among them) were prepared (and their future colleagues are still being prepared) for their vocation by specialized study after not more than two years of general education in college, followed, after four years of college, by the intensely specialized study required for the Master's or Doctor's degree, which generally signifies research competence in a special field. Here again the practice is thought justified by the fact that most college programs, still retaining one form or another of the elective system, include many specialized subjects of instruction for which the competent teacher is assumed to be one who has specialized in that subject.

This, then, is the prevailing pattern of teacher-training. On the whole, the realist in educational controversy finds this pattern acceptable, with, perhaps, minor changes or improvements; it accords, in his view, with the reality of the educational situation in America. The idealists, as might be expected, disagree, and they disagree in a body, without distinction between the traditionalists and the modernists among them. To the extent that they present a united front, the reform they urge in the preparation of teachers corresponds to their advocacy of reform of the school system.

Insisting upon an undifferentiated general education—essentially liberal in character—for every child for as long as possible, they confront the existing practices in the preparation of teachers with a basic reorganization embodied in the following three proposals:

1. All future teachers, elementary, secondary, or collegiate, should have four years of liberal education up to the B.A. degree, unmixed with any specialized training in the field of education.

2. Specialized training in the field of education, following the award of the B.A. degree, should be supplemented by clinical training in the arts of teaching, comparable to medical internship.

3. Every teacher should be expected to carry his own liberal education forward throughout his teaching career, and the conditions of his employment should provide the opportunity as well as the encouragement to do so.

What would these changes mean in terms of the attractiveness—or the unattractiveness—of the teaching profession? The realist says that they would make teaching harder to enter and more demanding upon the teacher and therefore even less attractive than it is now. The idealist admits that Mary Smith would not be ready to teach until at least a year or two later than she is now; her financial need for the completion of her preparation might require public support. If, however, Mary Smith was temperamentally unsuited to teaching, her "internship" would disclose the fact if her course grades did not, and both she and the profession would be spared subsequent disappointment. Conversely, if Mary had a temperament unusually suitable for teaching, her capacity would be earlier recognized, to her own and the profession's benefit. She would have worked harder to become a teacher, but she would not be pigeonholed as she is now; whatever subject she was teaching, she could help develop the whole program for her school or school system in co-operation with her colleagues, whatever subjects they were teaching, since all of them would have a common background of liberal education designed to enable them to comprehend and communicate the general principles of all the major fields of learning.

The realist says that Mary goes into teaching to get a job and that the way to get more and better Mary Smiths is to pay them more money, not to make the job harder, and certainly not to talk about "common backgrounds" and "general principles." The idealist thinks better of Mary and wishes her something better than better wages. He says she would be a learned woman, under his plan, and, as she continued her studies (with time off to do so and, if necessary, at public expense) throughout her career, she would be recognized as a learned woman, with the consequent higher status for herself and her profession that neither of them now enjoys. The profession would be more attractive and therefore more popular, and therefore more selective, than it can now afford to be. To be —and to remain—a teacher would be a greater ambition than it is today.

The disputes concerning the character of the university—of the institution, that is, whose primary function is the advancement of learning—cannot be considered without reference to the role of science and scientific thinking in an industrial democracy. There are, however, two questions regarding the university that are highly relevant to the problem of the preparation of teachers: The first, indicated in Proposal 2, above, is: Should special training in the liberal arts, as the arts of teaching and learning, be given institutionally beyond the B.A. degree, along with specialized study of the technical subjects developed by the empirical sciences of education? And, if so, what should be done to make such training available at the graduate level, either in the university or elsewhere? The second question is this: Should the institutional preparation of teachers beyond the B.A. degree include a program of general education at the advanced level, leading to an appropriate degree comparable to the present M.A. and Ph.D., to certify comparable competence in general rather than specialized teaching? And, if so, how can such facilities for general education at the graduate level be provided by the university unless it undertakes to promote the advancement of learning in general as well as in specialized fields?

These two questions concern primarily the preparation of teachers for liberal arts colleges, but they are not without some relevance for teachers at the secondary and even perhaps at the primary levels. And, in so far as their implications involve the whole subject of education, they tend to elicit contrary answers from the realist and idealist camps, without reference to the traditionalist-modernist dispute among the idealists as to the content, method, and materials of liberal education. That dispute—the hottest argued of all the strictly educational questions—comes to a head in the controversy that goes far beyond the confines of education, the controversy as to the role of science and scientific thinking in the life, and therefore in the educational system, of a modern industrial democracy.

PART V

Underneath the Issues: The Age of Science

CHAPTER 15

Trouble in Utopia

John Dewey posed the problem:

> I see at bottom but two alternatives between which education must choose if it is not to drift aimlessly. One of them is expressed by the attempt to induce educators to return to the intellectual methods and ideals that arose centuries before scientific method was developed. . . . The other alternative is systematic utilization of scientific method as the pattern and ideal of intelligent exploration and exploitation of the potentialities inherent in experience. . . . There is at least this much agreement among intelligent persons of both schools of educational thought. The educational system must move one way or another.

Most—and, in some respects, all—of the issues in American education involve this controversy, which we have repeatedly mentioned and just as repeatedly deferred: the controversy over the role of science. The issue, as we shall soon see, is much larger than the phrase "the role of science" suggests; it would be more appropriate to speak of the impact of modern science upon the life and thought of the human race.

The American revolution of 1850–1950 produced an industrial nation. Without science there would be no industry, but this is not to say that the age of industry, which began at the end of the eighteenth century, is the same as the age of science. The early stages of the industrial era utilized the steadily developing techniques that went all the way back to the first scientific speculations of the Greeks and the Chaldeans. Long-established patterns of thought and belief were undisturbed, or only marginally disturbed. The age of science, in contrast, has shaken man right down to the bedrock upon which, over all the preceding centuries, he built all his attitudes and all his institutions. It is not, then, enough to ask what are the implications for education in an industrial democracy; it is necessary to locate that industrial democracy in the momentous context of the age of science. The effect of science, so viewed, upon educational thinking is more profound than that of either industrialization or democratization; the controversy it has engendered is more cataclysmic than all the other issues of American education together.

Unlike all the other issues we have discussed—including that between the aristocrats and the democrats—this one enjoys the peculiarity of beginning and ending in philosophy. The facts of the matter are, as always, important, but in this matter they serve only to illuminate the theories, not to govern them. It can be said a priori that this dispute will never be decided by any common method of discovery, because its decisive element is a view of the nature of life and of thought—of the nature of the universe as well as that of man, his genesis, his purpose, and his destiny. It goes to what the ancients called "first principles" —those which proceed from no other and from which all others proceed.

This is the issue between the modernists and the traditionalists at bottom. It is not surprising that it should be deeply philosophical, for on both sides are the educational reformers in America, and, as Dewey observes, "only slight acquaintance with the history of education is needed to prove that educational reformers and innovators alone have felt the need for a philosophy of education. Those who adhered to the established system needed merely a few fine-sounding words to justify existing practices." Only utopians quarrel about principles, because only utopians look to them; stand-patters simply stand pat. In the established educational system (if it may be called a system) the traditionalists and the modernists are the utopians.

The traditionalists have not been seen as reformers at all, up until very recently; their position tended, for many years, to be identified with the gerund-grinding education that was (and to a great extent still is) to be found in Europe in the classical schools. This was the system that, as Henry Adams saw it in mid-nineteenth-century Germany, "struck the systemless American with horror. The arbitrary training given to the memory was stupefying . . . and the feats that the boys performed, without complaint, were pitiable. No other faculty than the memory seemed to be recognized. Least of all was any use made of reason. . . . The German machine was terribly efficient. Its effect on the children was pathetic."

Thus the modernists, rising against a system in part transplanted from Europe, precede the present-day traditionalists as reformers in the history of American education. Their beginning may be pretty well located in the decade of the 1900's. John Dewey's *The School and Society* was published in 1899. Although Dewey was by no means the first critic of existing educational practices, his was the sharpest, the broadest, the most persistent, and the most influential voice. He is clearly the founder of the modernist movement, and it may be no accident that the twentieth century's leading American philosopher was essentially a philosopher of education.

The traditionalists did not appear on the scene in force until almost 1930, after the reforms urged by Dewey had produced a widespread effect, first on the experimental schools and then on a considerable area of the educational system as a whole. Probably no single American's thinking has ever affected American life as rapidly and as extensively as Dewey's, but the rise of the modernist movement, with all that it owes to Dewey, cannot be separated from the situation of the American social order of the time. The beginning of the present century saw democratization straining against the fetters of class division and economic privilege; it was the time of Bryan's "cross of gold," Teddy Roosevelt's "trust-busting," and Woodrow Wilson's "new freedom." Educational modernism was part and parcel of the nascent social reformism of the day. Similarly, the traditionalists arose in a social situation characterized by the boom of the late 1920's and its subsequent collapse—a situation marked by moral cynicism, political indifference, and a preoccupation with the biggest, the shiniest, and the newest marvel of material production.

To say that the two movements were products of their respective times would be to deny independent validity to either of them. The times evoked them; historically, the two periods, a quarter-century or so apart, were peculiarly ripe for the appearance of the two successive and contending reforms. But it is safe to say that the traditionalists would have revolted, in season or out, against the domination of the curriculum by current phenomena and parochial interests, calling, as traditionalists have from Plato to Mill to Hutchins, for the experience of the race as the basis for understanding the experience of the moment, for the knowledge of man as man as the basis for understanding the problems of men here and now. So, too, the modernists would have revolted, with or without support from their analysis of contemporary social conditions, against the rigid, formalistic classicism at which they leveled their attacks.

Indeed, the modernist attack has never been mounted more vehemently than it was by Herbert Spencer in his *What Knowledge Is of Most Worth* in 1860. Spencer denounced traditional education as "second-hand facts instead of first-hand facts" and pronounced it useless: "As the Orinoco Indian puts on his paint before leaving his hut, not with a view to any direct benefit, but because he would be ashamed to be seen without it; so, a boy's drilling in Latin and Greek is insisted on, not because of their intrinsic value, but that he may not be disgraced by being found ignorant of them." And it is Spencer—but it might have been Dewey a half-century later—who says: "The constant habit of drawing conclusions from data, and then of verifying those conclusions by observation and experiment, can alone give the power of judging correctly. And that it necessitates this habit is one of the immense advantages of science."

People being what they are, and educators being people, the attention of the contending parties in education tends to focus on the opponent's vices rather than his virtues. Since the appearance of the traditionalists at the height of modernist influence, each of the two bodies of reform has identified the other with whatever abuses or distortions of the other's position might be discovered in current (or even in ancient) practice. The dead classicism which the modernists attacked at the beginning of the twentieth century—and which they continue to attack—the traditionalists also attack as a corruption of traditionalist principles, a fact which does not discourage the modernists from maintaining that this corruption is the traditionalist position. With equal and opposite fervor, the traditionalists, in the second quarter of the century, identified (and continue to identify) the modernist position with "progressive education" characterized by the account of the little boy who came home from school and said to his mother, "Mom, I'm tired of having to do what I want to do; I want to learn how to read and write." (Dewey himself in 1938 repudiated extreme "progressivism" as a misunderstanding and overzealous application of his educational philosophy.) Laymen who believe that educators and philosophers are above such police-court polemics betray an altogether proper esteem of education and philosophy—and a childlike innocence of educators and philosophers.

The modernist-traditionalist quarrel has produced a whole vocabulary of lurid juxtapositions, and in some circles it has produced nothing else. When we encounter expressions like "book-centered," "teacher-centered," "curriculum-centered," "discipline-centered," "compulsory," "medieval," "mystic," and even "fascist," we may assume that we are hearing a hot-headed modernist characterizing traditionalism. And expressions like "child-centered," "interest-centered," "fact-centered," "personality-centered," "hand-minded," "presentist," "permissive," "emotionalist," and "faddist" are more often than not the terms ascribed to modernism by the bitter traditionalist. What is important here is that neither of the protagonists would accept, unqualified, any of his opponent's epithets.

The modernist position is discountenanced as a whole because, like all theories which have to be judged by their practice, it is susceptible to overzealous application, to deep-endism, to cultism. And the discountenancing is done by the traditionalist, who thus plays himself as well as his modernist opponent into the hands of the existing system, whose votaries do not care how or why every reform is discountenanced as long as it is discountenanced. So, too, the modernist ascribes the most pernicious possible perversions of traditional principles to the traditionalist position. And all the while the modernist would no more urge that school children be permitted to use hatchets on one another than the traditionalist would force Greek conjugations upon the young at pistol-point. But as long as each of them says that this is precisely what the other would do, each of them concentrating his fire on the other's efforts to rectify the prevalent horrors of American education, the horrors have a fairly good chance of remaining intact and the public as a whole uninterested.

The traditionalists and the modernists have a very real quarrel and a very fundamental one—but it is not with each other's caricature. We have to discover where the quarrel in fact lies and what its real relation is to the maturation of modern science. To do so, it may be helpful, given the polemical background of this particular dispute, to ask first where the quarreling parties agree, and whether their agreement is real or only apparent.

CHAPTER 16

The Appearance of Agreement

Professor Sidney Hook of New York University, taking the modernist position, enumerates the ends or objectives of liberal education as follows:

1. Education should aim to develop the powers of critical, independent thought.

2. It should attempt to induce sensitiveness of perception, receptiveness to new ideas, imaginative sympathy with the experiences of others.

3. It should produce an awareness of the main streams of our cultural, literary and scientific traditions.

4. It should make available important bodies of knowledge concerning nature, society, ourselves, our country and its history.

5. It should strive to cultivate an intelligent loyalty to the ideals of the democratic community.

6. At some level, it should equip young men and women with the general skills and techniques and the specialized knowledge

which, together with the virtues and aptitudes already mentioned, will make it possible for them to do some productive work related to their capacities and interests.

7. It should strengthen those inner resources and traits of character which enable the individual, when necessary, to stand alone.

Of these seven stated aims, the traditionalists as a whole would take issue only on the sixth, concerning the way in which liberal education should prepare the child for his vocational future. But when Professor Hook enunciates the means to be used to achieve these agreeable goals, it is at once evident that the traditionalists would not accept his means, nor would he accept theirs. Disagreement about means, when it is sporadic or incidental, is not of great significance, but when, as here, it is clear and consistent, it throws the argument back to the apparent agreement on aims or ends.

It is at this juncture, as we shall see, that the agreement is apparent and not real. The words the modernists and the traditionalists use in defining the purposes of liberal education may be identical, but the meanings attached to them are contradictory. As Professor Hook himself observes, men can reach actual agreement about the objectives of education "only insofar as they submit to a *common method* of resolving conflicts of value in specific situations. But it is at the point of method, i.e., the process by which ideals are themselves derived and evaluated, that they fundamentally divide."

It is at just this point that the modernists and the traditionalists do divide, revealing the real depth of their conflict. The modernist thinks that the method by which fundamental values are to be formulated and tested is identical with the method of empirical science; the traditionalist thinks that, for the formulation and testing of fundamental values in those fields (such as ethics and politics) whose end purpose is not knowledge or production but human action, another method entirely is required than that of empirical science. The dispute as to method goes to the heart of the controversy and will be treated later; but its appearance here reveals a real incompatibility as to ends.

The agreement on content or curriculum is likewise only apparent or, at best, negative. The two parties concur so generally in their criticism of the existing content of education that this concurrence may lead to the mistaken conclusion that their remedies are the same. The agreement was summarized by Dewey when he wrote, late in his career, that "some of us who disagree radically with the reasons given [by the traditionalists] for criticizing our present system, and equally radically with the remedy that is urged, agree that the present system (if it may be called a system) is so lacking in unity of aim, material, and method as to be something of a patchwork. We agree that an overloaded and congested curriculum needs simplification." *But:* "The standpoint from which criticisms are made, and the direction in which reform is urged, are worlds apart."

Here, as in the case of aims or goals, the real disagreement, sometimes concealed by common criticism of existing practices, lies in the fundamentally different views of science—of its role in thinking and in learning—taken by the traditionalists and the modernists. Dewey, speaking for the modernists, says of the traditionalists, "We differ profoundly from their belief that the evils and defects of our [educational] system spring from excessive attention to what is modern in human civilization—science, technology, contemporary social issues and problems." The traditionalist would not, of course, accept this easy statement of his position vis-à-vis the present system; he would, however, say that in his view the modernist's curriculum would emphasize "what is modern" at the fatal expense of what is perennial.

This disagreement on content may appear at first to be one of emphasis alone. But in terms of actual curriculums the two opposing emphases produce fundamentally different educational patterns. At the risk—indeed, the certainty—of gross oversimplification, we may say that the modernist tends to rob philosophy and mathematics for the empirical branches of science, and the traditionalist to rob empirical science for philosophy and mathematics; that the traditionalist stints the social studies in favor of the humanities, while the modernist, conversely, corner-cuts language and literature in favor of sociology, social psychology, and current affairs; in addition, that the modernist confronting generalities moves to details and the techniques of gathering and testing them, while the traditionalist, similarly confronted, moves in the opposite direction, to principles. This is, as we have said, a gross oversimplification and a libel on both positions. But in practice the domination of one or the other doctrine usually means two radically different courses of study—often in the same institution.

At first glance the disputants would appear to agree on the relative roles of the past and the present in liberal education. This apparent agreement is often obscured by the rabid disagreement voiced by the extremists in both camps. We are indebted to Dewey again for the characterization and repudiation of the two opposite extremes: the one that "the main, if not the sole, business of education is the transmission of the cultural heritage"; the other that "we should ignore the past and deal only with the present and the future." In their moderate forms the traditionalist is no better represented by the "cultural heritage" fixation than the modernist is represented by the policy of ignoring the past altogether.

Criticizing the modernist extremists, Dewey says that "by reaction to an opposite extreme, as unfortunate as it was probably natural under the circumstances, the sound idea that education should derive its materials from present experience and should enable the learner to cope with the problems of the present and the future has often been converted into the idea that progressive schools can to a very large extent ignore the past." Dewey's formula for a moderate course—"to make acquaintance with the past a *means* for understanding the present"—is echoed by the assertion of the traditionalist philosopher, Whitehead, that "the only use of a knowledge of the past is to equip us for the present." But on close examination we find that the traditionalists and the modernists do not really agree on this point, even when both their positions are moderate.

The reason for their ultimate disagreement about the study of the past is, again, their disagreement about the meaning of modern science. The traditionalist thinks that the philosophy, theology, and poetry of the past contain many truths applicable to present problems, in spite of the fact that their formulation did not result from the use of scientific method and even if their concepts antedated the terms of modern science. The modernist denies that this is possible. The formulations of a pre-scientific era may appear to be relevant to contemporary problems, but they would have to be reformulated in terms that would enable them to be tested by the scientific method before their reliability, or even their meaning, could be determined. The past, then, has little more than historical value for the modernist; it is incapable, in its very nature, of providing currently useful or significant knowledge. The consequence is that for the modernist the role of the past in liberal education is peripheral, while the traditionalist, refusing to separate the past from the present (or the future), would give it parity with the contemporaneous.

Thus the three points on which apparent agreement is sometimes seen prove, upon closer analysis, to be controversial. There is real disagreement between the traditionalists and the modernists—both of them holding the democratic and idealist positions—on aims or ends, on content, and on the use of the past. And at all three points the underlying issue is the meaning of science and scientific method. This is the rock on which, having sailed boldly out of the safe harbor of realism, the undermanned raft of reform is broken.

CHAPTER 17

The Modernist Position

The controversy between the modernist and the traditionalist arises from their flatly opposed views of the nature of inquiry, an opposition which, in turn, arises from differing concepts of the nature of reality and the nature of intelligence.

The scientific method of inquiry, says the modernist, is the only valid method for the formulation of statements that are significant for experience and that can be tested by experience. Dewey speaks of this method as

so inclusive in range and so penetrating, so pervasive and so universal, as to provide the pattern and model which permits, invites, and even demands the kind of formulation that falls within the function of philosophy. It is a method of knowing that is self-corrective in operation; that learns from failures as from successes. The heart of the method is the discovery of the identity of inquiry with discovery. Within the specialized, relatively technical, activities of natural science, this office of discovery, of uncovering the new and leaving behind the old, is taken for granted. Its similar centrality in every form of intellectual activity is, however, so far from enjoying general recognition that, in matters which are set apart as "spiritual" or "ideal" and as distinctively moral, the mere idea of it shocks many who take it as a matter of course in their specialized work.

It follows—if the method employed by the empirical sciences is the *only* valid method of inquiry—that philosophy must employ this method in the investigation of "matters which are set apart as 'spiritual' and 'ideal' and as distinctively moral"; if, that is, philosophy, like the natural sciences, is to have significance for experience. What Dewey calls "reconstruction in philosophy" is a radical transformation of the philosophical enterprise from what it was in the pre-scientific age. In the age of science the task of the philosopher, recognizing the central position of the scientific method for all forms of inquiry, is to perfect that method by a critical formulation of its canons and to use it himself in dealing with the problems of philosophy.

Two immense consequences flow from this proposition. The first is the discontinuity between the new philosophy and the old. The second is the continuity between value (as the object of philosophical inquiry) and fact (as the object of natural science).

Except for historical or critical purposes, the whole tradition of pre-scientific thought can be ignored. Its ideas or theories or doctrines or arguments are worth studying only for insight into their relevance to the conditions of the pre-scientific culture of the undemocratic, non-industrial past. Such "truths" as the pre-scientific tradition may contain—in germ or by accident—must be reconstructed by a scientific and empirical philosophy before they become hypotheses that can be tested and applied.

The modernist would seem to be taking as his slogan the apostolic injunction, "Prove all things," if it were not for his healthy skepticism of all doctrines reached, like the Apostle's, by non-empirical method. The twentieth-century American lives in a world unimaginable by the pre-Christian Greek or the pre-*Mayflower* Christian. The world, in the process of being remade by man, remade him. This remade man made tools to meet his and his world's new needs. The modernist is not attacking old or ancient philosophies or theologies; he is only insisting that they be tested by modern man's modern instruments in the modern situation.

"Our adverse criticisms of the philosophies of the past," says Dewey, "are not directed at these systems with respect to their connection with intellectual and moral issues of their own time and place, but with respect to their relevancy in a much changed human situation. The very things that made the great systems objects of esteem and admiration in their own socio-cultural contexts are in large measure the very grounds that deprive them of 'actuality' in a world whose main features are different to an extent indicated by our speaking of 'the scientific revolution,' the 'industrial revolution,' and the 'political revolution' of the last hundred years." The educational implications of this position are inescapable: education must go either "backward to the intellectual and moral standards of a pre-scientific age or forward to a greater utilization of scientific method in the development of the possibilities of growing, expanding experience."

Given the exclusive validity of the scientific method, matters which have been set apart as philosophical now merge with the scientific. The homogeneity of such fields as physics and biology, on the one hand, and ethics and politics, on the other, necessarily follows from the use of the same method of inquiry. The discovery of values, value judgments, or ideals, ethical or political, is not differently achieved than the discovery of facts in the natural sciences. Ideals, like facts, arise in experience and must be submitted to empirical verification in terms of their practical consequences. Ethical and political theories, if they are to be anything more than empty gymnastics or sermonizing disguised as reasoning, have to be treated like hypotheses in the natural sciences, as formulas that function to direct investigation, not to conclude it.

Here again we can do no better than to quote John Dewey: "Educational theory or philosophy . . . must contest the notion that morals are somehow wholly separate from and above science and scientific method," and show that "principles and general truths in morals [are] of the same kind as in science—namely, working hypotheses that on one hand condense the results of continued prior experience and on the other hand direct further fruitful inquiry whose conclusions in turn test and develop for further use the working principles used."

This view has great appeal outside the field of education. It calls, in the conduct of business, government, personal relations, all the everyday affairs of life, for open-minded insistence on the evidence, an attitude geared to motion and a willingness to give the new a trial. All received dictates, from whatever authority, are questionable. Nothing is taken for granted, nothing in the realm of experience is accepted on "blind faith." If something is to be done or not done, it must be because experience indicates its workability or unworkability, not because it was once done or not done somewhere else under conditions no longer obtaining. Fixity is unrealism. Change—in the observed and in the observer—is the central fact of life.

Modern man must either be up-to-date or die clinging to dogmas irrelevant to the world he lives in. Experience—always in the process of being re-evaluated—is not only the best teacher; it is the *only* teacher, its curriculum trial and error, its school the fabled College of Hard Knocks. Knowledge is its fruit, knowledge tentatively held (like the conclusions of science), subject always to further validation or invalidation by the refining process of further experience. In this view alone, says the modernist, is human progress possible; in this spirit alone are fear and failure chastised, adventure and discovery invigorated, and man's high hopes sustained.

Adherence to scientific method, with its crucial consequences for education, is engendered by the philosophical modernist's conceptions of reality and intelligence. He holds that there is no meaning to such terms as "reality," "existence," "nature," or, of course, "truth," apart from their reference to aspects of experience. Outside of experience, or behind it, they signify nothing. They are not the ultimate objects of knowledge; knowing takes place within experience and serves merely as a bridge from past to future experience. It is a continuing process, just as experience itself is. The philosophies of the past, says Dewey,

have represented themselves as dealing with something which has variously been termed Being, Nature, or the Universe, the Cosmos at large, Reality and Truth. Whatever names were used, they had one thing in common: they were used to designate something taken to be fixed, immutable, and therefore out of time. . . . Into this state of affairs there recently entered the discovery that natural science is forced by its own development to abandon the assumption of fixity and to recognize that what for it is actually "universal" is *process;* but this fact of recent science still remains in philosophy, as in popular opinion up to the present time, a technical matter rather than what it is: namely, the most revolutionary discovery yet made.

Educationally, the crux of this discovery is the ultimacy of experience: "Experience as an active process occupies time. Its later period completes its earlier portion; it brings to light connections involved but hitherto unperceived. The latter outcome thus reveals the meaning of the earlier. . . . Every such continuous experience or activity is educative, and all education resides in having such experience."

From this view of the educative process it follows that the mind is not a faculty for knowing the features of an independent reality but a biological instrument which, like other vital organs of the body, functions to maintain and advance the living process. When the mind is engaged in knowing, it is operating not only within experience but *upon* experience, for knowing is itself productive of changes in experience. Hence learning, and, therefore, education, is "that reconstruction or reorganization of experience which adds to the meaning of experience, and which increases ability to direct the course of subsequent experience." Intelligence, far from being a faculty for laying hold of truths, is "a short-hand designation for great and ever-growing methods of observation, experiment, and reflective reasoning which have in a very short time revolutionized the physical and to a considerable degree the physiological conditions of life, but which have not yet been worked out for application to what is itself distinctively and basically *human*."

CHAPTER 18

The Traditionalist Position

Because Dewey himself is the author of the philosophy upon which his educational theories rest, it is possible to delineate the modernist position in terms of its origin and development from principles beyond those of education (for example, the nature of the mind). True, the philosophical views behind the modernist position have deep and elaborate roots in the past, in Comte, Hegel, Hume, Locke, and Bacon, to name only a few of their sources; but their application to education is, on the whole, new and, in Dewey and his associates and followers, original. The traditionalist position in education has no such sharply defined development in the present. Its exponents are numerous, influential, and many of them (more in England than in America) are eminent, but the position draws its arguments from so many quarters that it is easiest to present in generalized form.

Where the modernist asserts the exclusive validity of the scientific method, the traditionalist maintains that there are many valid methods of inquiry, each appropriate to its own subject matter. All these methods have certain fundamental features in common—objectivity, intellectual honesty, care and precision in methodology, and the aggregation and consideration of all available evidence. If the word "scientific" is taken to mean no more than these characteristics of procedure, then every valid method of inquiry is scientific. But the traditionalist more often uses the term as the modernist does, in its narrow sense of empirical or experimental investigation.

In this sense of the term, the traditionalist divides valid methods of inquiry into two large groups, in one of which the method of empirical science is the archetype. But some of the methods of this group—which, in the traditionalist's view, includes historical and philological research—utilize controlled conditions and some do not, some require the associated efforts of other fields of inquiry and some do not, and so on. The method of the chemist, which is adequate for questions in his own field, cannot answer the kind of question that confronts the astronomer; no more is the method of the physician adapted to building bridges or the method of the engineer to curing diseases. But all of them, including the historian and the philologist, use one or another of the methods of discovery in the modernist's sense.

In contradistinction is the group of methods used by mathematics, philosophy, and theology. If investigation may be said to be the common characteristic of the first group, reflection (and, perhaps, discussion) may characterize the second, although the traditionalist would also use the terms "speculative thought," "insight," "analysis," and so on. His is popularly called "the armchair method" in contrast to "the laboratory method," and if the armchair is thought to be less powerful or precise than the laboratory, the traditionalist would remind his opponent that the great instruments of precision and power—including nuclear power—are the end products of the mathematician's armchair.

The traditionalist does not mean that experience plays no part in the methods of the mathematician, the philosopher, and the theologian, any more than the modernist means that reflective thinking plays no part in empirical research. But the distinction is still clear between what for brevity may be called "the investigative method" and "the reflective method" if it is remembered that the former uses special, specially controlled, or specially arranged experiences as its materials, while the latter uses the common experience of mankind.

If philosophical investigation is to be conducted by a method different from that of science, then there is no necessity for a reconstruction of philosophy in an age of science—at least, not in so far as method is concerned. Philosophical inquiry must take account of new scientific knowledge, but the method by which the philosopher does his own characteristic work is unaffected. Neither the tremendous development of empirical science nor the application of its methods to new fields of inquiry alters the relationship of philosophy and science, although the clarification of that relationship may become more difficult and more important.

The traditionalist denies that modern science is exclusively modern. The scientific enterprise characterizes the whole Western tradition, not just its last few hundred years, and, however it may differ today from yesterday in the variety and accuracy of its instruments, it is the same in all epochs as regards both its methods and its general field of inquiry. Even as regards its instruments, they, too, are the product of growth, beginning with the wheel and the lever, in spite of the fact that at some point in this growth a combination of the developments up to that time produced a colossal acceleration. On this view there is no essential discontinuity between the "scientific" and the "pre-scientific" ages. The virtues of the scientific method were as highly regarded in their field in primitive science as they are today. The oath the modern physician takes was prescribed by Hippocrates in the fourth century before Christ.

What is uniquely modern about modern science, says the traditionalist, is not science itself but the modernist's attitude toward it. The real difference between a culture that is "modern" or "scientific" in this sense and the "pre-scientific" culture of the past is to be found in the fact that the modernist in philosophy has abandoned the method of philosophy for that of science. In short, the traditionalist would not call ours "the age of science" as if science were itself new, but, rather, the age of scientism or positivism, to the extent that the positive sciences have been taken as the only valid source of knowledge and their method as the only valid method of learning.

The assertion that there are sources of knowledge and methods of learning other than science and the scientific has two consequences that widen the breach between the traditionalist and the modernist. The first is that the intellectual tradition may contain truths that are still true, judged by the criteria of philosophical inquiry. The second is that practical wisdom or knowledge of moral values cannot be acquired in the same way as scientific knowledge about matters of fact or real existence.

Given the continuity of philosophical method, the fact that truths were formulated in undemocratic and non-industrial societies of the past does not confine their relevance to life under such circumstances and preclude their validity for the life we live today. If the continuation of philosophical inquiry challenges past formulations, the truths it discovers would have been as relevant to the past as they are to the present; if, for example, slavery is philosophically indefensible today, the traditionalist holds that it was just as indefensible in ancient

Greece. Philosophy develops in a different way from science, but it is not different from science in respect to the independence of its conclusions from local environment or personal predilection.

The traditionalist, therefore, denies the modernist's presentation of educational alternatives, "backward to the intellectual and moral standards of a pre-scientific age or forward to a greater utilization of scientific method." The alternatives are, rather, between two cultures, one retaining both science and philosophy as separate but related areas of knowledge, each with its appropriate method, the other rejecting philosophy altogether in so far as it does not use the scientific method or accepting it as a body of tentative formulations arising from experience and changing with changing experience.

The traditionalist makes three claims for philosophy, two of which have already appeared: The first is that philosophy is knowledge, not opinion or conjecture, and that it has the validity of knowledge as much as science. The second is that philosophical knowledge is independent of the empirical sciences in that the latter's methods are incapable of answering philosophical questions or of refuting philosophical conclusions. The third is that philosophical knowledge is superior to empirical science both theoretically and practically—theoretically, in that it is concerned with the ultimate nature of things, whereas science is concerned with their phenomenal aspects; and, practically, in that it is concerned with directing human life and society to its ends or goals, while science is concerned with technological applications in the sphere of productivity for man's use en route.

It is in this last area—that of the practical—that values or ideals are found, and to which belongs the whole realm of moral philosophy (i.e., ethics, politics, and the first principles of jurisprudence, education, etc.). Because moral philosophy is practical thinking with regard to the ends of life and society, it has a logic that is different from that of the theoretical branches of philosophy (such as metaphysics or the philosophy of nature) as well as from the logic of science. Practical judgments, judgments of what should be done, are inherently different from theoretical judgments or judgments of fact, judgments of what is. Therefore moral problems, although their solution proceeds in part by the "armchair" method of all philosophy, cannot be solved in the same way as those either of the theoretical branches of science or of their technological applications to production.

Affirming what the modernist denies, that "morals are somehow wholly separate from and above science and scientific method," the traditionalist does not assert that moral philosophy is something separate from or above theoretical philosophy. On the contrary, he holds that moral principles can be established only in terms of the nature of things as they are; that, before we can know what should be done, we have to know what is and what is possible. In other words, moral philosophy cannot be separated from reality, whose ultimate lineaments are the province of theoretical philosophy. Thus the traditionalist, in arguing for moral philosophy, maintains that its claims are rooted in reality, in what is, as firmly as are the scientist's.

It is not, however, the scientist with whom the traditionalist is arguing but the modernist. And the argument, having proceeded from the method to the content of learning, continues, necessarily, to the views of reality and intelligence which give rise to the modernist's espousal of the scientific method as uniquely valid.

Motivated, perhaps, by polemical considerations, the traditionalist accuses the modernist of being non-scientific as regards the nature of reality. The world not only moves and changes but exists and has to exist in order to move and change. The reality of the universe and the natures of the things in it are entirely independent of man's changing experience of them, even though it is through his experience of them that man comes to know and think about them. All forms of knowing (even mathematics) arise from sense experience; but this, the traditionalist insists, is not equivalent to saying that all knowing takes place within experience, if "within" means that knowing has no reference to things beyond experience, that is, to what the natures of things are, not merely to what they are experienced as.

True, human experience is a process in time; true, too, the world is a world of change and of changing things. But the world has permanent as well as mutable characteristics. As the traditionalist sees it, the modernist's exclusive reference to experience reduces all reality to process, the whole universe to flux.

There is more to life, says the traditionalist, than the individual's experience. There are the things—real things—he experiences, the stone walls he hits his head against, the storms and the calms, birth, marriage, death, the laws he finds immutable as well as the laws he makes and breaks. More than that, there is the experience of man, *Homo sapiens*, in which every individual participates and by which he is known to be a man. Man, whoever, wherever, whenever, however he is, confronts love and hate, ambition and abnegation and despair, hope, terror, envy, sacrifice, betrayal, temptation, satiety, trust and mistrust, pleasure and pain, death and the dream of eternal life. Man past, present, and future is man still, and only a species mutation will change his problems and the character of his struggle with them. There *is* such a thing, says the traditionalist, as human nature.

The traditionalist agrees with the modernist that in so far as education can be related to the child's experience it will be more interesting and more effective. But he sees things which in their very nature lie outside childhood experience and yet belong to the preparation of the young for adult life. The moral and political problems that beset the adult are either wholly outside the child's experience or within it only in rudimentary form. The child may have to make what for him are terrible choices; but he cannot have to choose between dishonor and death, or integrity and starvation, though in a hard world he may some day have to. There may not be martyrs and saints and heroes in a given schoolroom or in a given town or even in a given country or a given decade, but mankind may need martyrs, saints, and heroes a decade later. How is the child in such circumstances to have experience of them so that, if he will not be one of them himself, he will at least know one when he sees him, and not mistake him for a rogue or a fool? Where in the experience of childhood except through the study of the past is the child in such circumstances to acquire "the habitual vision of greatness"?

Their preoccupation with change led the early-twentieth-century modernists to proclaim, in Dewey's words, that "the educative process can be identified with growth." But in 1938, in his *Experience and Education*, Dewey took note of the traditionalist objection that "growth is not enough; we must also specify the direction in which growth takes place, the end toward which it tends." His reply to the traditionalist complaint that "a man may grow in efficiency as a burglar, as a gangster, or as a corrupt politician" was:

From the standpoint of growth as education and education as growth the question is whether growth in this direction promotes or retards growth in general. Does this form of growth create conditions for further growth, or does it set up conditions that shut off the person who has grown in this particular direction from occasions, stimuli, and opportunities for continuing growth in new directions? What is the effect of growth in a special direction upon the attitudes and habits which alone open up avenues for development in other lines? I shall say that when and *only* when development in a particular line conduces to continuing growth does it answer to the criterion of education as growing.

The traditionalist is dissatisfied with "more growth" as the answer to his objection that "growth" is an inadequate end for education. "If," says the French philosopher Jacques Maritain in his *Education at the Crossroads*, "the teacher himself has no general aim, nor final values to which all this process is related; if education itself is to grow 'in whatever direction a novelly emerging future renders most feasible'; then it teaches educational recipes but gets away from any real art of education: for an education which does not have any goal of its own and tends only to growth itself without 'end beyond further growth,' is no more an art than an art of architecture which would not have any idea of what is to be built, and would only tend to the growth of the construction in whatever direction an addition of new materials is feasible."

When, says the traditionalist, to the doctrine of "continuing growth" is added the modernist's insistence that values, aims, or ends are to be tested by scientific method and by scientific method alone, the modernist presents us with an amoral education for amoral men in an amoral world. "It is not science, but men, that have purposes," says Robert Hutchins, "and they do not get them from science." The phraseology is modern, the point extremely ancient. "They are wise to do evil," said Jeremiah of his countrymen, "but to do good they have no knowledge." "Did you never observe," Socrates asks in Plato's *Republic*, "the narrow intelligence flashing from the keen eye of a clever rogue—he is the reverse of blind, but his keen eyesight is forced into the service of evil?" And while Alexander Hegius, the fifteenth-century religionist who taught Erasmus, was saying that learning is pernicious "if it is acquired at the expense of piety," his contemporary, the ribald satirist Rabelais, was saying, "Science without conscience is the ruin of the soul."

The traditionalist's position would be inconsistent if, arguing as he does that there is an objective reality beyond experience and change, he did not maintain that there was a faculty for knowing that reality. The mind, in the traditionalist view, is not identical with the brain, although it cannot function without the brain; it is not a biological instrument like the sensitive faculties that man shares with the other animals; it is a distinctively human faculty or capacity, one that man alone possesses. The traditionalist agrees with the modernist that the mind maintains and advances the life-process, but he asserts that this function is derivative from the essential ability to reason, to abstract from common experience a comprehension of the nature of things. The realities are there, and the mind, in knowing them, does not alter or affect them, although one application of its knowledge may be productive, that is, the transformation of matter through the useful or industrial arts.

But the highest realities accessible to the mind—highest in the sense of universality and in the order of causation—are the natures of things and the practical precepts that are generated by the understanding of these realities. Learning has reference to experience, both past and future, but this is not its sole reference. Education, as the traditionalist sees it, is not, then, merely "the reorganization or reconstruction of experience." It is the actual acquisition of actual understanding about actual things, above all those things whose primacy, in themselves and for the achievement of the ordered life and the just society, entitles those who pursue them to the ancient appellation of lovers of wisdom.

Like the modernist, the traditionalist is giving voice to a whole outlook on life, not just to a philosophy of education. His slogan might not be, "The more things change, the more they are the same," but it would embody some such spirit. It might be, "There is nothing *entirely* new under the sun." He would be as likely to enter the shop that advertised "Tried and True" as the modernist would be to patronize the merchant whose sign read "Tried and Still Being Tried." A democratic idealist, like the modernist, he might be said to be more conservative psychologically. Through the process of all experience the traditionalist discerns an unbroken—and unbreakable—thread of continuity.

In everyday life the traditionalist position is reflected in a preoccupation with the long view. Its proponent is not an enthusiast for novelty as such; whatever novelty presents, he thinks that he has seen something somehow like it somewhere in the prior history of the human race. He is slower to hail progress than some of his neighbors, who may regard him as, at best, a corrigible optimist. He is not a big buyer of new books on bringing up children or getting peace of mind. He does not trade in his car—or his Weltanschauung—very often. Politically, he is likely to be a universalist, because he sees in all men an essentially common and an essentially constant nature. But by the same token, he is not easily convinced that anything better than Beulah Land or worse than the Flood is just around the corner.

Along with the modernist (and the Apostle) the traditionalist says, "Prove all things," but he thinks that the experience of the ages adds weight to proof. He is likelier than the modernist to add to the injunction (as the Apostle does), "Hold fast that which is good."

CHAPTER 19

The Educational Consequences

It is clearer now why the democratic idealists, divided as they are on the nature of knowledge, of knowing, and of reality, are at greater odds among themselves than they are with either the aristocrats or the realists. The traditionalist-modernist split affects every aspect of the educational system, beginning with the aim and content of basic schooling.

That the aim of education is profoundly affected by the issue scarcely needs saying when we reflect that one party regards the mind as a biological instrument for directing process and reorganizing experience, while the other regards it as a faculty primarily engaged in the pursuit of knowledge and wisdom. The difference regarding aim is further deepened by the alternative conceptions of knowing—on the one hand, as something that takes place entirely within experience and serves as a bridge from past to future experience and, on the other, as an apprehension of the permanent features of an independent reality and of the natures of things as they are.

But the difference is deepest with respect to educational content or curriculum. The role which the study of the past is to play differs, necessarily, according to different judgments of the significance of the past to the present. For the modernist the thought of the past is, as we have seen, primarily of historical and critical interest; for the traditionalist it is, in addition, the accumulating repository of knowledge and wisdom which, especially in the non-empirical subjects, is valid apart from time and place, is as new as today's science, and is an inherent part of the experience of every human being.

On means and method, too, the disputants differ radically. While they agree that liberal education consists, at least in part, in the discipline or habituation of the mind to clear and critical thinking, their agreement ends at this point. The modernist thinks that training in the scientific method (and, perhaps, in semantics) is all that is required to discipline the intellect, while the traditionalist believes that all the liberal arts are required, those involved in discussion and analysis as well as those involved in research and discovery.

The quarrel extends, naturally, to the study of science itself. There is no difference about the amount of time or attention each party would allot to science in the curriculum; if anything, the traditionalist would require more science than the modernist. St. John's College, at Annapolis, offering a traditionalist education, is the only liberal arts college in America that demands four years of laboratory science of every student; it takes literally the glorious Latin pun that serves as its college motto: *Facio liberos ex liberis libris libraque*, "I make free men out of boys by means of books and balances."

The difference between the traditionalist and the modernist at this point lies entirely in the way each would organize the study of science for the purposes of general education, in contrast to specialized study in a particular field. The traditionalist thinks that the great documents of science, including records and reports of historic investigations (even those that contain errors long since corrected), are indispensable for a general and liberal comprehension of the development of science to its present place and power, as well as of the scientific aspect of the Western tradition as a whole. The modernist would serve the purpose by experience with contemporary science, in both study and experimentation.

These differing approaches to the organization of scientific study reflect a difference regarding teaching methods as a whole. The modernist would have teaching follow the model of empirical scientific research, while the traditionalist would have it use all the methods presented by the variety of valid types of inquiry which he distinguishes, of which empiricism is only one. Then, too, the modernist, because he regards knowing as a process that affects or alters the object known (and therefore as essentially productive or practical), tends to assimilate knowing to doing and to universalize this tendency in the principle that all learning is by doing. From this principle arise the various forms of the "project method" or "activity programs" of education.

From this principle, too, arises the modernist's emphasis on interest as the motivating factor in education. The traditionalist agrees that the child's interest facilitates his learning; indeed, in his argument with the realist on the question of unequal educability, he makes the point that much apparent inequality is nothing but the teacher's failure to stimulate the interest of the "backward" child. But he maintains that interest is *a*—not *the*—motivating factor in learning. Another, he says, is authority, the rightful, reasoned authority of parents and teachers exercised wholly for the benefit of the child.

The modernist is a little uneasy at this kind of talk; more

than a little, perhaps, and in his extreme form he raises the cry of "authoritarianism." But the traditionalist insists that there are things that every child has to learn before he can be interested in them; things that we have to learn although we may *never* be interested in them. "He who will not answer to the rudder," says the traditionalist, drawing upon the words of tradition, "will answer to the rock." There is a less formidable way of saying it: We cannot wait to become interested in brushing our teeth before we are taught to do it.

The modernist view is not modern; Martin Luther, in the sixteenth century, wished that the studies of the young at school could be so organized that the scholars might take as much pleasure in them as in playing ball all day. But life, says the traditionalist, is not all a ball game (or a ball), and neither is learning, even in childhood. If the most interesting teacher alive is unable to interest Johnny in mathematics in the first grade, the second, the third, or even the fourth or fifth, Johnny's mathematical education may be deferred temporarily; but he had better learn to count up to ten before he is graduated from Harvard, even if he remains mathematically uninterested.

There are things that are interesting to children (and to adults) that are important; there are others, the traditionalist reminds the modernist, that are unimportant, and still others that are harmful. A poll presented to a recent convention of the National Association of Secondary School Principals revealed that teen-age students want more knowledge of good manners, good grooming, how to date, marriage problems, sex education, and child psychology and care. The speaker presenting the poll also disclosed that four out of five parents wanted "family life" taught in the schools. One Chicago parent-teacher group thought that instruction on how to choose the right mate should be given.

Apart from the problem (itself interesting) of teaching the young how to choose the right mate, the consequence of teaching the things the young would like to be taught may be the elimination of the things that the young ought to be taught. The modernist, insisting that the school experience be acceptable to the child, has perhaps been more effective in this area than in any other; his unrelenting attack on the rote-learning of materials which the child cannot identify with his own life has produced a great nation-wide reform in teaching technique. But the traditionalist reminds the modernist of their common commitment, as democratic idealists, to the principle that the same quality of education be given every child and of their common hostility to the dilution of the curriculum by job-training. May not a tendency to focus our efforts on the child's interest jeopardize quality and "water the soup" of education?

The Fairfield, Connecticut, Citizens' School Study Council report on its two-year study said: "One sort of problem arises from unwitting misuse and abuse of some of the widely accepted philosophical assumptions now underlying American public education—such as the aim of 'teaching the whole child,' of making school a happy place, and of teaching children through experiences they have had in common. The end results of these distortions have been that some children have not mastered essential skills; that many children understandably prefer lurid comic books and television shows to insipid, goody-goody school readers; and that pupils are taught to conform rather than to be individuals." Fostering the interest of the individual child in important subject matter is one thing; appealing to his interest on the lowest-common-denominator basis of "doing" in a childhood group is another.

The traditionalist agrees with the modernist's contention that all learning depends primarily upon the activity of the learner. But he does not think that this means that all learning is by doing, unless, of course, the word "doing" refers to every conceivable form of human activity. In that sense, one can say that we learn mathematics by "doing" mathematics. But if "doing" signifies overt social behavior having some practical or productive intent, then it is only one form of human activity. Just as one learns how to behave socially by actions of a social kind, so one learns to read by reading and to think by thinking.

The modernist may reply that "learning by doing" means engaging in the process of inquiry itself, modeled on the pattern of scientific method. It involves the inquirer in doing something about his experiences in order to learn something from them. The traditionalist would still deny that all learning is by doing in this sense, because he denies that all learning is patterned upon the scientific method. Learning by discussion, for example, is not learning by doing in the sense that the scientific method is either employed or acquired in the process.

It is this dispute about the relationship of knowing and doing that underlies, finally, the traditionalist-modernist disagreement about the vocational aspect of education. According to Dewey, "intelligence is best exercised within activity that puts nature to human use," and this doctrine is the basis for his advocacy of education through occupations.

Education through occupations combines within itself more of the factors conducive to learning than any other method. . . . It has an end in view; results are to be accomplished. Hence it appeals to thought; it demands that the idea of an end be steadily maintained, so that activity must be progressive, leading from one stage to another; observation and ingenuity are required at each stage to overcome obstacles and to discover and readapt means of execution.

This view has its basis in Dewey's espousal of scientific method. The method of "putting nature to human use" is for him at once the method of science and the method of industrial production. Thus it is necessary—and possible—to integrate vocational with liberal education in an industrial and scientific civilization. The traditionalist, disagreeing on method, mind, knowledge, and the learning process, sees in the character of our civilization no reason whatever for diluting liberal education with vocational elements. Again reminding the modernist of their common democratic opposition to job-training in the name of education, he maintains that "education through occupations" has an ineluctable tendency to become occupational training.

Turning from liberal education itself to the education of teachers and the advancement of learning, we find that the issue between the traditionalists and the modernists has fundamental consequences in these areas, too. The differences in viewpoint arising from differing concepts of liberal education are easily discerned.

The traditionalist would give future teachers a more intensive training in the liberal arts, as the arts of teaching and learning, than can be obtained at the undergraduate level. In his view, something like the degree of Master of Arts, if it signified some mastery of these arts beyond the baccalaureate, might be required to certify competence in teaching. The modernist, on the other hand, recommends specialization in some field of scientific research as the best way to acquire a mastery of what for him is the one valid method of teaching and learning, that is, the empirical method. And, since education has itself become a field of empirical research, the modernist thinks that the teacher in training can acquire much of the necessary discipline by studying educational methods and problems in schools of education.

Disagreeing right to the bitter end—not captiously, but because of the incompatibility of their views of science and scientific method—the two parties to the dispute would organize the advancement of learning each on his own principles. On the whole, the modernist here moves in the direction of the realist, accepting the university as it now is, with its intense degree of specialization of the sort required for scientific research. He would, to be sure, like to improve its procedures, tighten its structure, and (in common with the traditionalist) eliminate some of the antics that infect the university by way of the college—but all this for the purpose of more intensive specialization to serve the further advancement of learning in an age of science. The traditionalist, insisting that truth is found by different methods appropriate to different subject matters, sees continual synthesis of findings as the indispensable condition of the advancement of learning as a whole and, therefore, as one of the central functions of the university. He rejects the notion that specialization should be the exclusive occupation of scholars and the sole organizing principle of the institution; he sees *diversity* in the modernist's university, but he does not see *unity* in it.

It is precisely at the point where he quarrels with the modernist that the traditionalist thinks learning cries loudest for advancement. What *is* learning? How is it achieved, and, if in more than one way, why? What is the intellect, and what is its relation to experience? What is the nature of reality, and man's relation to it? These, the two parties to the dispute agree, are the most general of general questions and the most basic of basic issues. They are philosophical—on any view of philosophy—and profoundly so. It is questions of this order that must, in the traditionalist's view, be answered before learning, and not just parts of learning, can be advanced. The university, if it generalized its specialists, might bring the traditionalist and the modernist together and resolve not only the greatest issues in education but the greatest issues in philosophy and science.

PART VI

Roads to Resolution

CHAPTER 20

Stripping for Action

There is no point in arguing facts and still less in arguing suppositions of fact. The preliminary problem in controversy is to discriminate between issues of fact—issues which are ultimately controlled and resolved by the accumulation and analysis of all the relevant circumstances and conditions—and issues of principle. Issues of fact settle themselves when the facts are known and faced. Many of the bitterest disputes in American education would yield to the facts without further effort, if the facts were known. In so far as they are accessible, educators have only themselves to blame for continued confusion; but it may not be amiss to observe that the confusion itself, the disorganization (or unorganization) of education in America, perhaps precludes making a start.

Facing the facts is something else. On the whole, and certainly in so far as the issues are controversial, this is a political and not an educational problem. Education in the United States is controlled by the citizenry, and it is they who will decide whether or not to accept the reforms indicated by the facts, once the facts are before them. Here, in the realm of political decision, the educator can perhaps educate the public, but, again, the public will decide whether or not it is willing to listen to the educator or, indeed, whether or not he is to have a voice. There may be a considerable quarrel—a political, not an educational, quarrel—about the proper location and division of the control of education in a democracy. But this much is certain, wherever the control is thought to reside: No democratic society will accept reforms (or even changes, whether or not they are reforms) in its educational system against which it feels very strongly. It can only be hoped, as a manifestation of democratic faith, that, once the facts are known to the public, the public will decide well. But first the facts must be discovered.

Issues of principle—although here, too, the public will make the decisions in a democracy—are different. No principle contrary to relevant circumstances and conditions can ever be sustained, but many issues of principle are not exhausted by even the fullest knowledge of the facts. Pushed far enough back, principles are philosophical convictions. The traditionalist would say that these convictions are demonstrable by philosophical methods; they are not mere opinions, prejudices, speculations, or conceits. The modernist would demand their demonstration by empirical methods. And so, in a sense, the problem of distinguishing fact from principle plunges us back into the traditionalist-modernist argument, and, unless the two can find a meeting ground, we should be proceeding by begging the very essence of the question.

One interpolation here: The process of stripping the issues for action, of finding not resolution but ground for arguing resolution, requires "coming to terms." This problem was examined at the beginning of this book; it need only be referred to here. Unless the parties to the argument are using the same words in the same way, they are not arguing with one another. We have attempted in this discussion—certainly with partial success at best—to avoid both "loaded" and ambiguous expressions, or to emphasize the exact manner in which they are "loaded" and to clear them, for purpose of the discussion, of ambiguity. But the problem remains, and always will; without it human discourse would be perfect and misunderstanding impossible; and men are not perfect, and the mind operates through the imperfections of man's senses and the obscurities and diversions of his feelings. What the disputants can do is to be always acutely aware of the problem, both of them bent, co-operatively, on speaking the same language in so far as it is given men to speak it.

To the resolution of the great controversy over the role of science and scientific method, we can bring the obvious conclusions that, to the extent that their positions are contradictory, either the modernist is right, and the resolution should be in favor of adopting his views as well established, or the traditionalist is right, and the resolution should be in favor of adopting his views as well established, or the issue between them is far from settled by the arguments thus far advanced (or, at least, pursued) on either side. The first two conclusions would be unprofitable, from the standpoint of argument, and, where they raise the issue of the extent to which their underlying concepts are already well established, they would plunge us into the third conclusion in any case.

The pursuit of the resolution would then involve a constructive reconsideration of whatever in the whole tradition of Western thought bears upon the controversy. The reason that examination of the tradition is indispensable is not merely because the traditionalist's views have an elaborate ancestry in that tradition but also because the position of the modernist (as only the extremist would deny) also has many antecedents of its own in the tradition, near and remote.

How well established are the principles underlying the argument about science? For many centuries the traditionalist position (or some variant of it) was taken as established for once and all. There is still a widespread impression that the traditionalist is the dogmatist who harks blindly back to the authoritarian temper of a pre-scientific age, while the modernist is, perhaps, as widely thought to cherish the tentativeness of science and to suspend judgment while theories are weighed and hypotheses tested. But the common view yields to closer examination of the two positions, at least in American education. "Nothing is more curious," says Whitehead in *The Philosophy of John Dewey*, "than the self-satisfied dogmatism with which mankind at each period of its history cherishes the delusion of the finality of its existing modes of knowledge. Skeptics and believers are all alike. At this moment the scientists and the skeptics are the leading dogmatists."

However willingly one accepts or rejects Whitehead's assertion, it is quite clear that, where discussion of the philosophy of education occurs, the philosophy on which the modernist proposals are based is advanced as being as well established as the traditionalist position was once thought to be. This phenomenon appears plainly in Dewey's own dismissal of any and all traditional philosophical views as irretrievably conditioned by the circumstances of the undemocratic, non-industrial, and pre-scientific cultures of the past. One thing is certain. If either of these positions—the traditionalist or the modernist—can as a whole be well established as a result of genuine controversy, it should prevail in the theory and practice of education in America. As educational idealists, both the modernist and the traditionalist are devoted to variety. This does not mean that they are devoted to chaos. (If they were, they would both of them approve of the present school system.) Nor does it mean that they are devoted to variety for the sole sake of variety. They both want the best possible kind or kinds of education for every American child and adult.

The discovery of the best kind or kinds of education calls for more than the facts. It calls for a continuous and systematic process of discussion, carried on in a manner adequate to the difficulty of the task. For the central issues in education regarding the place of science and philosophy are not issues of fact in any readily ascertainable sense of that term; they are the deepest possible issues of principle. "The final chapter of philosophy," says Whitehead in his essay on Dewey, "consists in the search for the unexpressed presuppositions which underlie the beliefs of every finite human intellect. In this way philosophy makes its slow advance by the introduction of new ideas, widening vision, and adjusting clashes. . . . Philosophy should aim at disclosure beyond explicit presuppositions. In this advance, Dewey himself has done noble work."

Noble work remains to be done, perhaps the noblest, in the form of organized confrontation of the whole complex of fundamental questions in education. It can be undertaken by experts and by laymen, and best, it may be, by both together. For common sense plays as large a role in the most fundamental disputes as does special knowledge. If the work is undertaken with a preliminary effort to separate issues of fact from those of principle, with resources adequate to discovering the facts, and is then carried forward with mutual respect by the disputants for one another and, above all, for the principles of disputation itself, there is no inherent reason why further advance cannot be achieved.

CHAPTER 21

Fact and Principle: A Recapitulation

There remains one task more in setting forth the issues in American education, and that is to re-examine them briefly to determine, at least tentatively, which appear most likely to yield to fact and which must be pursued, in whole or in greater part, on the basis of principle.

The greatest issue of all—that between the modernist and the traditionalist—seems most clearly to lie within the area of principle. At least the facts involved are facts of so general and abstract a character that the assembling of specific data to support the two positions does not look like a promising venture. The nature of man, for example, is not likely to be discovered in the same way as the incidence of an epidemic disease or the division of political opinion before an election.

Proceeding in reverse order from the one with which this

discussion moved as a whole, to the issues regarding adult education, the education of teachers, and the advancement of learning, we are already aware that these three areas of argument are intimately involved with the philosophical dispute regarding the role of science and scientific method. On the whole, the realists are ranged on one side, either acquiescent or enthusiastic in support of existing practices, and the idealists (including the traditionalists and the modernists) on the other. The traditionalists and the modernists stand together in their criticism of existing practices on the basis of their principles of what education should be in an industrial democracy, but they fall out in regard to the character of the reforms they urge, on the basis of their radically opposed principles of what education should be in an age of science. Facts, largely unassembled and very largely unanalyzed, play a role, especially in the disputes regarding adult education and the education of teachers, but the role is obviously secondary to issues of principle.

The issue of vocational education is next. This is the issue that divides the idealists from the realists, who accept or approve differentiation, with vocational training for some and liberal education for others after a limited amount of common schooling. But this is the issue that also divides the idealists into modernists, who think that vocational elements, integrated with liberal education, should have a direct bearing on the occupational aspects of modern life, and the traditionalists, who would exclude any direct dilution of liberal education. Is the issue here one of fact or of principle? To the extent that it turns on the nature of the mind and the process of learning and knowing, we have already seen that it is one of principle. But if differing concepts of the relation of labor and leisure are also involved, the issue may also be one of fact.

The modernist charges the traditionalist with two errors that are vestiges of the aristocratic, pre-industrial past. The first is the view, prevalent in antiquity, that labor is degrading, especially manual or productive labor. The second is the related view that labor is for the sake of leisure, implying that leisure is the noble or honorable part of life and that it is appropriate to the more noble and honorable natures among men. The traditionalist charges the modernist with failing to see that the eradication of the separation between working and leisure classes in society, accompanied by a growing respect for labor, does not alter the principle that in all essential respects labor is indeed for the sake of leisure and that leisure is indeed better than labor in every man's life.

The parties to the argument seem to agree that the social and human gains resulting from industrialization greatly outweigh the disadvantages, however serious the problems it has engendered. They seem to agree, further, that among the principal gains are the eradication of the division between laboring and leisure classes and the provision of the decencies of life and leisure for more men.

On the relevant principles, too, they seem to be agreed. The modernist as well as the traditionalist accepts the sense in which all labor is compulsory, involving an element of drudgery from which leisure is free. And the traditionalist, as well as the modernist, says that, to whatever extent the character of labor is intrinsically rewarding to the worker (in addition to its purely external compensation), to that extent the activities involved in labor do not differ essentially from those of leisure.

Both parties know that many forms of labor in an industrial economy present the drudgery of monotonous and impersonal work, with none of the intrinsic satisfaction of the instinct of workmanship that tends to assimilate labor to leisure. Knowing this, both of them think that liberal education should serve the vocational aspect of human life by doing whatever it can to humanize or liberalize all forms of labor in an industrial economy.

How, then, do the traditionalist and the modernist differ?

Despite their mutual polemics, their great difference would seem to be with regard to the means each proposes as the way to make liberal education discharge its responsibility to the vocational aspect of life. And the issue about means would seem to involve only questions of fact, answerable by the testing of different policies in practice. Can vocational and liberal education be successfully integrated? If they can be, would their integration be the most effective and direct means to the end of humanizing or liberalizing labor? If the answers appear to be available experimentally, the charge upon education, as regards this issue, is clear: it must experiment.

We come, now, to the issue of equal educational opportunity for all, on which the realists, accepting the prevailing practice of differentiation, disagree with the idealists. On the realist view, the principle of equal opportunity is maintained if all children receive the same amount of schooling, while the idealist maintains that differentiation (providing different kinds of schooling after a basic period) is incompatible with the principle.

The resolution of the issue would seem to lie partly in fact and partly in principle. The principle involved is whether the equality of all men as persons is an equality of kind and not of amount, and whether, conversely, their inequality is one of amount and not of kind. If, as the idealist maintains, the one human equality is of kind and not of degree, and the many human inequalities are of degree and not of kind, the idealist argument would prevail; and vice versa. But here, again, the "facts" are essentially analytical and not assimilable on a common fact-gathering basis; the issue appears, in other words, at this level to be one of principle. But when the realist replies that the facts of human inequality make it impossible to give every child the kind of education the idealist proposes, and the idealist questions these facts (or at least their educational significance), the road to resolution requires sustained and intelligent experimentation to determine whether an undifferentiated program is in fact possible.

The impossibility of giving every child a liberal education might raise questions as to the validity of universal suffrage, that is, of democracy itself, and so we are led to the last issue in American education (or the first issue with which we dealt), the issue of democracy and aristocracy. In one sense, the issue is of little practical consequence for education, partly because the aristocrats are so small in influence and partly because, as they themselves observe, they are calling for a basic political change, to which the educational reforms they urge would be only incidental. The fact is that in our present society—and in the foreseeable future—the practical problems of education concern its improvement in an industrial democracy. Yet it is worth spending a moment on the issue itself, "academic" as it is, for democratic education presupposes the acceptance of democratic government.

The point at issue is the soundness in principle of political democracy, and particularly of its central tenet, universal and equal suffrage. If the majority—or even a minority—of men do not have the capacity for citizenship and should not, therefore, be granted a voice in their own government, it can certainly be argued that they do not have the capacity or the need for anything more than rudimentary education or training. But this issue turns on a deeper issue: the nature of human equality.

If all men are equal as persons (in contrast to things) and if, therefore, none is to be used to serve another's purpose, then and then only can the principle of political democracy be upheld. But we are required here to go to an antecedent question, arising from the terms we are using. What is a person? What is a thing? What, if anything, distinguishes them? Is a catatonic schizophrenic a person, possessed (whether or not he knows it) of certain rights which in justice belong to all persons and only to persons? Is the most brilliant chimpanzee ever trained in a laboratory a thing, to be used for the purposes of persons? Facts would be relevant to the resolution of these issues, underlying all other issues in politics or education; but the ultimate answers are theoretical, if anything at all is theoretical.

The American revolution of 1850–1950 has produced conditions that have radically altered education and educational questions. The new circumstances of this new kind of society have overwhelmed us with new facts, some of the most crucial of which, in education, we have not taken time to assemble or assimilate. But whatever the facts are, there are issues of principle still, and theoretical criteria on which the facts must be tentatively or firmly judged. Faith in the kind of society we are trying to produce in America is not a faith in facts alone but in an idea of a way of living and dying. It is supposed that the best education, even if it is not explicitly designed to serve that idea, will nevertheless serve it because the idea is the best idea. To the extent that the search for the best education persists, the search for the best society persists; and in the measure that the best education is achieved will the best society be achieved.

Acknowledgment

Acknowledgment

The authors wish to acknowledge their heavy indebtedness to William J. Gorman for his basic contributions to the thought and organization of this book, and to the following friends and colleagues for their advice and assistance in different stages of its preparation: Robert C. McNamara, Jr., Ralph W. Tyler, Louise Butler van Peski, and Lynn A. Williams, Jr.

Bibliography

Bibliography

I

XENOPHON (*ca.* 430–355 B.C.)

The Education of Cyrus (Cyropedia). Trans. H. G. DAKYNS. "Everyman's Library." New York: E. P. Dutton & Co., 1914.

PLATO (*ca.* 427–*ca.* 348 B.C.)

The Republic, Books vi–vii. In *The Dialogues of Plato,* Vol. I. Trans. B. JOWETT. 2 vols. New York: Random House, 1937.

Meno. Ibid.

Laws, Books ii and vii. *Ibid.,* Vol. II.

ARISTOTLE (384–322 B.C.)

Metaphysics, Book i. In *The Basic Works of Aristotle.* Ed. R. MCKEON. New York: Random House, 1941.

Ethics, Books i–vi. *Ibid.*

Politics, Books vii–viii. *Ibid.*

CICERO, MARCUS TULLIUS (106–43 B.C.)

De oratore. Trans. E. W. SUTTON and H. RACKHAM. 2 vols. "Loeb Library." Cambridge, Mass.: Harvard University Press, 1942.

SENECA, LUCIUS ANNAEUS (*ca.* 4 B.C.–*ca.* A.D. 65)

Seneca's Letters to Lucilius. Trans. E. P. BARKER. Oxford: Clarendon Press, 1932.

QUINTILIAN (MARCUS FABIUS QUINTILIANUS) (*ca.* A.D. 35–*ca.* 95)

Institutes of Oratory, Book i. Trans. H. E. BUTLER. 4 vols. "Loeb Library." Cambridge, Mass.: Harvard University Press, 1921.

PLUTARCH (*ca.* A.D. 46–120)

Lycurgus (in *The Lives of the Noble Grecians and Romans*). In *Great Books of the Western World,* Vol. XIV. Chicago: Encyclopaedia Britannica, 1952.

"A Discourse Touching the Training of Children." In [*Moralia*] *Plutarch's Morals.* Ed. W. GOODWIN. 5 vols. Boston: Little, Brown & Co., 1871.

SEXTUS EMPIRICUS (second century A.D.)

Outlines of Pyrrhonism. In *Sextus Empiricus.* Trans. R. G. BURY. 3 vols. "Loeb Library." Cambridge, Mass.: Harvard University Press, 1933.

AUGUSTINE (SAINT) (A.D. 354–430)

The Confessions, Book i. In *Great Books of the Western World,* Vol. XVIII. Chicago: Encyclopaedia Britannica, 1952.

On Christian Doctrine, Book ii. *Ibid.*

Concerning the Teacher. In *Basic Writings of St. Augustine,* Vol. I. Ed. W. J. OATES. 2 vols. New York: Random House, 1948.

CASSIODORUS SENATOR, FLAVIUS MAGNUS AURELIUS (*ca.* A.D. 490–*ca.* 583)

[*Institutiones*] *An Introduction to Divine and Human Readings.* Trans. L. W. JONES. New York: Columbia University Press, 1947.

AQUINAS, THOMAS (SAINT) (A.D. 1225–74)

Concerning the Teacher. In M. H. MAYER, *The Philosophy of Teaching of St. Thomas Aquinas.* Milwaukee, Wis.: Bruce Publishing Co., 1929.

II

ERASMUS, DESIDERIUS (*ca.* 1467–1536)

De pueris statim ac liberaliter instituendis (*On Liberal Education*).
Trans. in W. H. WOODWARD, *Desiderius Erasmus Concerning
the Aim and Method of Education.* Cambridge: Cambridge University Press, 1904.

The Education of a Christian Prince. Trans. L. K. BORN. New
York: Columbia University Press, 1936.

CASTIGLIONE, BALDASSARE (1478–1529)

The Book of the Courtier. Trans. T. HOBY. "Everyman's Library."
New York: E. P. Dutton & Co., 1928.

MORE, THOMAS (SAINT) (1478–1535)

Utopia. Ed. H. GOITEIN. Trans. R. ROBINSON and F. BACON.
"Everyman's Library." New York: E. P. Dutton & Co., 1928.

LUTHER, MARTIN (1483–1546)

*To the Councilmen of All Cities in Germany That They Establish
and Maintain Christian Schools.* In *The Works of Martin Luther*,
Vol. IV. Ed. H. E. JACOBS. 6 vols. Philadelphia: A. J. Holman
Co., 1915–32.

ELYOT, SIR THOMAS (*ca.* 1490–1546)

The Governour. "Everyman's Library." New York: E. P. Dutton
& Co., 1937.

RABELAIS, FRANÇOIS (*ca.* 1490–1553)

Gargantua and Pantagruel, Book I. In *Great Books of the Western
World,* Vol. XXIV. Chicago: Encyclopaedia Britannica, 1952.

IGNATIUS OF LOYOLA (SAINT) (1491–1556)

The Constitutions. In *St. Ignatius and the Ratio studiorum.* Ed.
E. FITZPATRICK. Trans. M. H. MAYER. New York: McGraw-Hill
Book Co., 1933.

VIVES, JUAN LUIS (1492–1540)

On Education. Ed. and trans. F. WATSON. Cambridge: Cambridge
University Press, 1913.

MULCASTER, RICHARD (*ca.* 1530–1611)

Positions. London: Longmans, Green & Co., 1887.

Elementarie. Oxford: Oxford University Press, 1925.

MONTAIGNE, MICHEL DE (1533–92)

"Of the Education of Children" (in *The Essays*). In *Great Books of the Western World*, Vol. XXV. Chicago: Encyclopaedia Britannica, 1952.

LYLY, JOHN (*ca.* 1554–1606)

Euphues: The Anatomy of Wit; Euphues and His England. Ed. M. W. CROLL and H. CLEMONS. New York: E. P. Dutton & Co., 1916.

BACON, FRANCIS (1561–1626)

Advancement of Learning. In *Great Books of the Western World*, Vol. XXX. Chicago: Encyclopaedia Britannica, 1952.

New Atlantis. Ibid.

"Of Custom and Education." In *The Essayes*. "Everyman's Library." New York: E. P. Dutton & Co., 1932.

"Of Studies." *Ibid.*

COMENIUS, JOANNES AMOS (1592–1670)

The Great Didactic. Ed. and trans. M. W. KEATINGE. London: A. & C. Black, 1923.

DESCARTES, RENÉ (1596–1650)

Rules for the Direction of the Mind, Rules III, IV, and XIII. In *Great Books of the Western World*, Vol. XXXI. Chicago: Encyclopaedia Britannica, 1952.

Discourse on the Method, Part I. *Ibid.*

MILTON, JOHN (1608–73)

Of Education. In *The Works of John Milton*, Vol. IV. Ed. F. A. PATTERSON. 18 vols. New York: Columbia University Press, 1931–38.

LOCKE, JOHN (1632–1704)

Some Thoughts concerning Education. In *The Works of John Locke*, Vol. X. 10 vols. London: T. Tegg, 1823–24.

FÉNELON, FRANÇOIS DE SALIGNAC DE LA MOTHE- (1651–1715)

Adventures of Telemachus. Ed. O. W. WIGHT. Trans. DR. HAWKESWORTH. Boston: Houghton Mifflin Co., 1887.

A Treatise on the Education of Daughters. Ed. and trans. T. F. DIBDIN. Boston: C. Ewer, 1821.

SWIFT, JONATHAN (1667–1745)

An Essay on Modern Education. In *The Prose Works of Jonathan Swift,* Vol. XI. Ed. T. SCOTT. 12 vols. London: G. Bell & Sons, 1900–1914.

VOLTAIRE (FRANÇOIS MARIE AROUET) (1694–1778)

"University." In *A Philosophical Dictionary.* Ed. W. W. FLEMING. 10 vols. New York: F. R. DuMont, 1901.

FRANKLIN, BENJAMIN (1706–90)

The Autobiography of Benjamin Franklin, the Unmutilated and Correct Version. Ed. J. BIGELOW. New York: G. P. Putnam's Sons, 1927.

HUME, DAVID (1711–76)

An Enquiry concerning Human Understanding, Secs. I and VII. In *Great Books of the Western World,* Vol. XXXV. Chicago: Encyclopaedia Britannica, 1952.

ROUSSEAU, JEAN JACQUES (1712–78)

Émile. Trans. B. FOXLEY. "Everyman's Library." New York: E. P. Dutton & Co., 1933.

HELVÉTIUS, CLAUDE ADRIEN (1715–71)

A Treatise on Man: His Intellectual Faculties and His Education. Trans. W. HOOPER. 2 vols. London: Vernor, Hood & Sharpe, 1810.

SMITH, ADAM (1723–90)

An Inquiry into the Nature and Causes of the Wealth of Nations, Part V, chap. i, Arts. 2–3. In *Great Books of the Western World,* Vol. XXXIX. Chicago: Encyclopaedia Britannica, 1952.

KANT, IMMANUEL (1724–1804)

The Educational Theory of Immanuel Kant. Trans. E. F. BUCHNER. Philadelphia: J. B. Lippincott Co., 1904.

LESSING, GOTTHOLD EPHRAIM (1729–81)

The Education of the Human Race. Trans. F. W. ROBERTSON. London: C. K. Paul & Co., 1881.

GIBBON, EDWARD (1737–94)

The Decline and Fall of the Roman Empire. New York: P. F. Collier & Son, 1910.

JEFFERSON, THOMAS (1743–1826)

Memoirs, Correspondence, and Miscellanies from the Papers of Thomas Jefferson. Ed. T. J. RANDOLPH. Charlottesville, Va.: F. Carr, 1829.

PESTALOZZI, JOHANN HEINRICH (1746–1827)

How Gertrude Teaches Her Children. Ed. E. COOKE. Trans. L. E. HOLLAND and F. C. TURNER. Syracuse, N.Y.: C. W. Bardeen, 1915.

SCHILLER, (JOHANN CHRISTOPH) FRIEDRICH VON (1759–1805)

Letters upon the Esthetic Education of Man. In *Literary and Philosophical Essays.* "The Harvard Classics." New York: P. F. Collier & Son, 1910.

FICHTE, JOHANN GOTTLIEB (1762–1814)

Addresses to the German Nation, Addresses II–III, IX–XIV. Trans. R. F. JONES and G. H. TURNBULL. Chicago: Open Court Publishing Co., 1922.

RICHTER, JOHANN PAUL FRIEDRICH (1763–1825)

Levana; or, The Doctrine of Education. Boston: D. C. Heath & Co., 1886.

HERBART, JOHANN FRIEDRICH (1776–1841)

The Science of Education. Trans. H. M. and E. FELKIN. Boston: D. C. Heath & Co., 1902.

FROEBEL, FRIEDRICH WILHELM AUGUST (1782–1852)

The Education of a Man. Trans. W. N. HAILMANN. New York: D. Appleton Co., 1887.

FARADAY, MICHAEL (1791–1867)

Lectures on Education. London: J. W. Parker, 1885.

WHEWELL, WILLIAM (1794–1866)

Of a Liberal Education in General; and with Particular Reference to the Leading Studies of the University of Cambridge. London: J. W. Parker, 1880.

MANN, HORACE (1796–1859)

Lectures on Education. In MARY PEABODY MANN, *Life and Works of Horace Mann.* 5 vols. Boston: Lothrop, 1867–91.

Few Thoughts for a Young Man. Ibid.

NEWMAN, JOHN HENRY (1801–90)

The Idea of a University Defined and Illustrated. Ed. D. O'CONNOR. New York: America Press, 1941.

University Sketches. New York: Walter Scott Publishing Co., 1902.

EMERSON, RALPH WALDO (1803–82)

The American Scholar: An Oration Delivered before the Phi Beta Kappa Society, August 31, 1837. In *The Complete Essays and Other Writings of Ralph Waldo Emerson.* Ed. B. ARKINSON. "Modern Library." New York: Random House, 1940.

MILL, JOHN STUART (1806–73)

On Liberty, chap. ii. In *Great Books of the Western World,* Vol. XLIII. Chicago: Encyclopaedia Britannica, 1952.

Inaugural Address, Delivered to the University of St. Andrews, Feb. 1st, 1867. London: Longmans, Green, Reader & Dyer, 1867.

SPENCER, HERBERT (1820–1903)

Essays on Education and Kindred Subjects. New York: E. P. Dutton & Co., 1928.

ARNOLD, MATTHEW (1822–88)

Culture and Anarchy: An Essay in Political and Social Criticism. Ed. J. D. WILSON. Cambridge: Cambridge University Press, 1932.

NIETZSCHE, FRIEDRICH WILHELM (1844–1900)

On the Future of Our Educational Institutions. Trans. J. M. KENNEDY. In *The Complete Works of Friedrich Nietzsche,* Vol. III. Ed. DR. O. LEVY. 18 vols. London: T. N. Foulis, 1909–15.

III

ADAMS, HENRY BROOKS (1838–1918)

The Education of Henry Adams. "Modern Library." New York: Random House, 1941. (1st ed., Boston, 1907.)

BRYCE, JAMES (1838–1922)

The Function of a University. Adelaide, Australia: W. K. Thomas, 1912.

JAMES, WILLIAM (1842–1910)

The Principles of Psychology. In *Great Books of the Western World,* Vol. LIII. Chicago: Encyclopaedia Britannica, 1952.

PIUS XI, POPE (1857–1939)

Christian Education of Youth. In *Five Great Encyclicals.* New York: Paulist Press, 1939.

PEARSON, KARL (1857–1936)

The Grammar of Science. London: J. M. Dent, 1937.

VEBLEN, THORSTEIN BUNDE (1857–1929)

The Higher Learning in America: A Memorandum on the Conduct of Universities by Business Men. New York: B. W. Huebsch, 1918.

DEWEY, JOHN (1859–1952)

Democracy and Education: An Introduction to the Philosophy of Education. New York: Macmillan Co., 1931. (1st ed., New York, 1916.)

How We Think: A Restatement of the Relation of Reflective Thinking to the Educative Process. Boston: D. C. Heath & Co., 1933. (1st ed., Boston, 1910.)

Reconstruction in Philosophy. New York: Henry Holt & Co., 1920.

The School and Society. Chicago: University of Chicago Press, 1926. (1st ed., Chicago, 1899.)

The Sources of a Science of Education. ("Kappa Delta Pi Lecture Series," No. 1.) New York: Liveright, 1929.

Experience and Education. New York: Macmillan Co., 1938.

BURY, JOHN BAGNEL (1861–1927)

The Idea of Progress: An Inquiry into Its Origin and Growth. New York: Macmillan Co., 1932.

WHITEHEAD, ALFRED NORTH (1861–1947)

The Aims of Education and Other Essays. New York: Macmillan Co., 1929.

The Organization of Thought, Educational and Scientific. Philadelphia: J. P. Lippincott Co., 1917.

BUTLER, NICHOLAS MURRAY (1862–1947)
The Meaning of Education. New York: Charles Scribner's Sons, 1900.

BABBITT, IRVING (1865–1933)
Humanism. Providence, R.I.: Brown University Press, 1926.

WALSH, JAMES JOSEPH (1865–1942)
Education of the Founding Fathers of the Republic. New York: Fordham University Press, 1935.

CUBBERLEY, ELLWOOD PATTERSON (1868–1941)
Readings in the History of Education. Cambridge, Mass.: Riverside Press, 1920.

MEIKLEJOHN, ALEXANDER (1872——)
Education between Two Worlds. New York: Harper & Bros., 1943.

RUSSELL, BERTRAND ARTHUR WILLIAM (1872——)
Education and the Good Life. New York: Boni & Liveright, 1926.
Skeptical Essays, Essay XIV. New York: W. W. Norton & Co., 1928.
Why Men Fight: A Method of Abolishing the International Duel. New York: Boni & Liveright, 1930.

NOCK, ALBERT JAY (*ca.* 1873–1945)
The Theory of Education in the United States. Chicago: Henry Regnery Co., 1931.

EBY, FREDERICK (1874——)
The Development of Modern Education. New York: Prentice-Hall, Inc., 1952.

EBY, FREDERICK, and ARROWOOD, C. F.
History and Philosophy of Education: Ancient and Medieval. New York: Prentice-Hall, Inc., 1940.

GENTILE, GIOVANNI (1875–1944)
The Reform of Education. Trans. DINO BIGONGIARI. New York: Harcourt, Brace & Co., 1922.

LIVINGSTONE, SIR RICHARD WINN (1880——)
On Education. Cambridge: Cambridge University Press, 1944.

MARITAIN, JACQUES (1882——)
Education at the Crossroads. New Haven, Conn.: Yale University Press, 1943.

ORTEGA Y GASSET, JOSÉ (1883–1955)
Mission of the University. Trans. H. L. NOSTRAND. Princeton, N.J.: Princeton University Press, 1944.

PINKEVITCH, ALBERT PETROVITCH (1884——)
The New Education in the Soviet Republic. Trans. NUCIA PERLMUTTER. Ed. GEORGE S. COUNTS. New York: John Day Co., 1929.

RANK, OTTO (1884–1939)
Modern Education: A Critique of Its Fundamental Ideas. Trans. M. E. MOXEN. New York: A. A. Knopf, Inc., 1932.

BELL, BERNARD IDDINGS (1886——)
Crisis in Education. New York: McGraw-Hill Book Co., 1949.

RUGG, HAROLD ORDWAY (1886——)
The Teacher of Teachers. New York: Harper & Bros., 1952.

ARROWOOD, CHARLES FLINN (1887–1951)
Thomas Jefferson and Education in a Republic. New York: McGraw-Hill Book Co., 1930.

ELIOT, THOMAS STEARNS (1888——)
Notes towards the Definition of Culture. New York: Harcourt, Brace & Co., 1949.

ULICH, ROBERT (1890——)
History of Educational Thought. New York: American Book Co., 1945.
Crisis and Hope in American Education. Boston: Beacon Press, 1951.

RUSSELL, WILLIAM FLETCHER (1890——)
How To Judge a School. New York: Harper & Bros., 1954.

BERKSON, ISAAC BAER (1891——)
Education Faces the Future. New York: Harper & Bros., 1943.

RICHARDS, IVOR ARMSTRONG (1893——)
  Interpretation in Teaching. New York: Harcourt, Brace & Co., 1938.

CONANT, JAMES BRYANT (1893——)
  On Understanding Science. New Haven, Conn.: Yale University Press, 1947.

  Education in a Divided World. Cambridge, Mass.: Harvard University Press, 1948.

VAN DOREN, MARK ALBERT (1894——)
  Liberal Education. New York: Henry Holt & Co., 1943.

KELLEY, EARL CLARENCE (1895——), and RASEY, MARIE I. (1887——)
  Education and the Nature of Man. New York: Harper & Bros., 1952.

BRUBACHER, JOHN SEILER (1898——)
  A History of the Problems of Education. New York: McGraw-Hill Book Co., 1947.

  Modern Philosophies of Education. New York: McGraw-Hill Book Co., 1950.

HUTCHINS, ROBERT MAYNARD (1899——)
  No Friendly Voice. Chicago: University of Chicago Press, 1936.

  The Higher Learning in America. New Haven, Conn.: Yale University Press, 1936.

  Education for Freedom. Baton Rouge, La.: Louisiana State University Press, 1943.

  The Democratic Dilemma. Uppsala, Sweden: Almquist & Wiksells, 1952.

  The Conflict in Education. New York: Harper & Bros., 1953.

  The University of Utopia. Chicago: University of Chicago Press, 1953.

HOOK, SIDNEY (1902——)
  Education for Modern Man. New York: Dial Press, 1946.

TYLER, RALPH WINFRED (1902——)
  Basic Principles of Curriculum and Instruction. Chicago: University of Chicago Press, 1950.

FINE, BENJAMIN (1904——)
Democratic Education. New York: Crowell-Collier Co., 1945.

BRAMELD, THEODORE BURGHARD (1904——)
Patterns of Educational Philosophy. New York: World Book Co., 1950.

YAUCH, WILBER ALDEN (1904——)
How Good Is Your School? New York: Harper & Bros., 1951.

CHALMERS, GORDON KEITH (1904——)
The Republic and the Person. Chicago: Henry Regnery Co., 1952.

HILGARD, ERNST ROPILQUET (1904——)
Theories of Learning. New York: Appleton-Century-Crofts, 1956.

HIGHET, GILBERT (1906——)
The Art of Teaching. New York: A. A. Knopf, Inc., 1950.

GRISWOLD, ALFRED WHITNEY (1906——)
Essays on Education. New Haven, Conn.: Yale University Press, 1954.

BARZUN, JACQUES MARTIN (1907——)
Teacher in America. Boston: Little, Brown & Co., 1945.

WOODRING, PAUL (1907——)
A Fourth of a Nation. New York: McGraw-Hill Book Co., 1957.

BUTLER, JAMES DONALD (1908——)
Four Philosophies and Their Practice in Education and Religion. New York: Harper & Bros., 1951.

BESTOR, ARTHUR EUGENE (1908——)
Educational Wastelands. Urbana, Ill.: University of Illinois Press, 1953.
Restoration of Learning. New York: A. A. Knopf, Inc., 1955.

POUSSON, LEONARD BERNARD (1913——)
The Totalitarian Philosophy of Education. ("Philosophical Studies," Vol. LXXX.) Washington, D.C.: Catholic University of America, 1944.

PRESIDENT'S COMMISSION ON HIGHER EDUCATION
  Higher Education for American Democracy. Washington, D.C.: Government Printing Office, 1947.

UNIVERSITY OF CHICAGO
  The Idea and Practice of General Education. Chicago: University of Chicago Press, 1950.

HARVARD COMMITTEE
  General Education in a Free Society. Cambridge, Mass.: Harvard University Press, 1951.

Index

Index

Adams, H., 7, 14, 147
Adams, J., 4
Adult education
  aristocrat view of, 122–23
  as contemporary problem, 29, 45, 46, 122
  controversy on, 45, 121–27
  democrat view of, 123
  effect on school system, 121–32
  equal opportunity for, 122–23, 128
  existing practices in, 129–30
  idealist view of, 123–26
  institutions for, 29, 40, 46
  liberal character of, 123–26, 128
  majority view of, 129–30
  modernist view of, 126
  nature of, 120–21, 125, 127–28
  preparation of teachers for, 42, 53
  program for, 46, 127–29

  realist view of, 123
  techniques of, 41
  traditionalist view of, 126
Advancement of learning, 23, 42, 53–54
Antioch College, 101
Aquinas, T., 23
Aristocrat
  on adult education, 122–23
  (ancient), on human inequality, 72–74
  controversy with democrat, 71–77, 122–23
  (modern), on human inequality, 74–75, 77
  as term in educational controversy, 67–68
Aristotle, 18, 24, 83
  affirmed educational tradition, 21
  on educational goals, 15